SPIRITUAL LESSONS

FROM

LITERARY MASTERS

BY

EDWIN L. WEAVER

ZONDERVAN PUBLISHING HOUSE

GRAND RAPIDS - - - - - - - - - - - - - MICHIGAN

Printed in United States of America

EIGHT-FIFTEEN FRANKLIN ST.
GRAND RAPIDS - - - MICHIGAN

FOREWORD

WHEN Izaak Walton wrote his *Lives,* the secular emphasis was less common but nowadays the makers of literature are seldom treated from a religious point of view. In each of the following chapters the writer seeks some outstanding lesson propounded or illustrated in the life and writings of an author. Consequently a complete and many-sided presentation is not intended. Accuracy in the handling of facts is not disregarded, nor are the spiritual needs and interests of young people, for whom these essays were especially written. The major writings of the various authors under consideration and standard biographies and works of critical comment were used, and to these I am indebted for material. Bibliographies are not added, for they can readily be found in works of scholarly pretensions. Originally these essays, and others not included in this book, were written in response to the request and encouragement of Clayton F. Yake, Scotdale, Pennsylvania, and appeared in religious periodicals for Christian youth. They are now made available in a permanent form.

E. L. WEAVER.

CONTENTS

		PAGE
I.	IN THE BEGINNING *Caedmon*	7
II.	THE GREATER LOYALTY *George Herbert*	13
III.	DILIGENCE REWARDED *Henry Wadsworth Longfellow*	20
IV.	IDEAL FRIENDSHIP *John Milton*	25
V.	THE CHARM OF OLD THINGS *Washington Irving*	30
VI.	DEEP IN HUMILITY *John Woolman*	36
VII.	THE CHARM OF COMMON THINGS *William Wordsworth*	43
VIII.	LIVING IN THE WOODS *Henry David Thoreau*	51
IX.	LOVE NOT THE WORLD *Christina Rossetti*	58
X.	CALM WOODS AND STILL WATERS *William Cullen Bryant*	64
XI.	TRIFLES MAKE PERFECTION *Thomas Gray*	70
XII.	CONQUERING THROUGH PATIENCE *Louisa May Alcott*	76
XIII.	A GALLERY OF PORTRAITS *William Law*	82
XIV.	THE FIFTH COMMANDMENT *Thomas Carlyle*	89
XV.	THE USE OF IDEAS *Ralph Waldo Emerson*	97
XVI.	AT THE SHRINE OF BACCHUS *Robert Herrick*	104
XVII.	THE ART OF LOVING GOD I *Richard Rolle*	109
XVIII.	THE ART OF LOVING GOD II *Richard Rolle*	114
XIX.	BEAUTY INVISIBLE *Nathaniel Hawthorne*	121
XX.	GLEANINGS FROM AN ANECDOTE MONGER *Thomas Fuller*	128
XXI.	IS DEATH THE GOAL OF LIFE? *Percy Bysshe Shelley*	135
XXII.	THE CONSECRATION OF TALENT *Harriet Beecher Stowe*	141

SPIRITUAL LESSONS
===== FROM =====
LITERARY MASTERS

BY
EDWIN L. WEAVER

I

IN THE BEGINNING
CAEDMON

THIRTEEN centuries ago there were no United States of America and what we know now as the English language was not in existence. Millions of books at present in the libraries of the world were then unwritten, but we do have poetry written near that time by Caedmon, the earliest English poet. Missionaries had already carried the gospel to the British Islands, so that the primitive tribes knew some of the same Bible stories that we know. The Christian religion, which has colored English literature for many centuries, had a prominent place in some of our earliest recorded songs.

Caedmon, said to have been a herdsman, was not educated and had never learned any poetry, although when this story took place he was already considerably advanced in years. People enjoyed entertainment and music in those days as well as now, and Caedmon often attended a feast in the evening. At those feasts it was the custom to request each person to sing in turn while someone played the harp and in this way promote mirth for the entertainment of the group. Whenever Caedmon saw the harp come near him, he felt ashamed because he thought he could not sing; so he arose from the feast and went home.

On one particular night each person was again supposed to sing. When Caedmon saw that his turn would soon come, he left the house of entertainment as usual but went this time to the stables where the charge of horses had been committed to him for that night. After a while he stretched himself on a bed and fell asleep. Soon he dreamed that a stranger came to him, greeted him by name, and said, "Caedmon, sing me something."

He answered, "I cannot sing; for the reason I left the entertainment and retired here is because I cannot sing."

The stranger spoke to him again and said, "Yet you could sing."

"What shall I sing?" asked Caedmon.

The stranger replied, "Sing to me the beginning of all things."

On receiving this answer, he at once began to sing in praise of God the Creator in verses and words he had never heard before. When he awoke from sleep, he remembered all that he had sung.

The next morning Caedmon related the dream to the steward, or farm bailiff, under whom he worked. The latter persuaded him to go to a monastery and tell his dream there. Accordingly he went to the monastery at Whitby, where the abbess, Hilda, in the presence of many learned men, had him tell his dream and repeat the verses so that they could test his powers. They all concluded that God had conferred on him a heavenly grace. These scholarly monks explained some portion of sacred history and asked him to render it into verse. He soon transformed it into excellent poetry, and the abbess, recognizing that the illiterate herdsman had received a gift from heaven, urged him to abandon his worldly calling and become a monk. With her request he complied, became an inmate of the monastery, and throughout the remainder of his life turned into poetry whatever he could hear and learn from the explanation of Scriptures by the learned monks. His poetry consisted of the sweetest songs; its music was so delightful that even his teachers wrote down the words from his lips and learned them.

Only sacred themes were used in his verse. He began with the story of the creation of the earth and of man as told in Genesis; then wrote about the departure of the people of Israel from the Land of Egypt, their entrance into the Promised Land; and various other Old Testament narratives. From the New Testament he wrote about Christ's incarnation, death, resurrection, and ascension into heaven, the coming of the Holy Spirit, and the teaching of the Apostles, and composed many songs about the day of judgment, the terrors of hell, and the kingdom of heaven.

Since Caedmon recognized that he did not learn the art of poetry from men but that it was the gift of God, he could never compose any trivial or vain poem. He composed only such songs as his pious tongue could fitly sing and which were in praise of the Creator. Worthy he was of divine favor, for he was a very religious man, submitted himself to religious discipline, and served God with a pure mind and undisturbed devotion. The unvarying aim of his poetry was to turn men from the love of sin to the love of righteousness. This end was achieved, for he caused many to despise the world and turn to God.

As well as for the place he holds in the history of literature, Caedmon is distinguished for setting an admirable standard before the makers of literature.

Through the centuries following his, some authors have appeared equally consecrated to a holy use of the literary art. Others have altogether ignored the glory of God in their efforts.

Many a creator of literature has lived in a realm of carnal, material, or worldly ideas. Although he may have penetrated deeply into the reasonings of the mind, he never discovered the wealth of spiritual truth revealed only to the true Christian. There are noted works utterly lacking in Christian elements. "He became a free-thinker in religion"; "he prided himself on his paganism, his rebellion against the very spirit of Christianity"; these are a few statements made in recent years with reference to gifted English poets. Such authors gave God no credit for their talent; indeed they used their gifts in opposing Him, instructing contrary to His teachings, and pleasing the evil minds and perverted tastes of men.

Other writers, drinking from fountains of worldly wisdom while at the same time reading the divinely inspired Scriptures, have an intellectual conception of spiritual truth but have not desired the indwelling Holy Spirit. As extensive readers they have absorbed ideas from the classical works of the Greeks and Romans, the tales and philosophies of the pagan Orient, and the meditations and doctrines of the Church Fathers. By the fusion of materials from these and other sources, masterpieces were built. The finished product often has a Christian coloring but is essentially non-Christian. Such authors lack a definite faith in Christ.

There are writers whose hearts have been opened to the reception of Christ as Savior. Theirs has been an attitude of faith and an act of consecration. Because art has been dedicated to a heavenly purpose, the products are not the wood and stubble that shall be burned, but the gold and precious stones that shall abide.

Writings thoroughly Christian and at the same time truly classic include some of our hymns. The Olney hymns of Cowper are the work of a true poet, the product of a believing soul. Watts wrote with a true poetic inspiration; to Christ all his powers were consecrated, and he has told us that his is a purer flame than that of the popular pagan love poetry. Some of the religious verse of Whittier has received an honored place in our hymnals.

A body of Christian literature, some of which has taken permanent form in print, has come from the pulpit. Sermons of literary and spiritual power were delivered by Hugh Latimer, an English farmer's son who during Reformation times preached before kings and kept audiences breathless by his striking manner of expression. Because of the imaginative and artistic qualities of his sermons, Jeremy Taylor has been designated the "Shakespeare of the pulpit." John Donne preached sermons noted for their rhetoric and erudition.

That literary gifts should be consecrated to God's service has been the conviction of many poets. The Anglo-Saxon writers of verse, newly converted from paganism, followed the example of Caedmon and specialized in Christian poetry. The work of George Herbert, a lover of the church, is thoroughly Christian. Henry Vaughan, almost a contemporary of Herbert, turned from secular thoughts to spiritual and put his meditations into poetic form. The chief interest in the life of Christina Rossetti was the Christian religion, and her poetic inspiration came from her faith. Numerous poems distinctly Christian are scattered through the writings of European and American poets.

The Christian classics are humble and unpretentious. They must be sought, but they have rich stores of recorded experience awaiting cultivation. Not only in hymns, sermons, and in various forms of verse, but also in biography, autobiography, fiction, essays, journals, diaries, and letters, have been expressed the thoughts of the pious who recognized God as the giver of talent, dedicating themselves to art as to a holy work. These have written on sacred or reputable themes with the high purpose of exalting truth, honoring God, and rendering service to humanity. Thus have they followed the example set by Caedmon in the beginning.

II

THE GREATER LOYALTY

GEORGE HERBERT

IN a small parish with twenty cottages and less than a hundred souls, lived and labored two centuries ago an humble and devout parson, a servant of the church, designated as "one of the holiest men in Christendom." But he had not been ever thus. Not many years before he had been a highborn, learned, and accomplished official of the university and of the government. By surrender to the divine Will he advanced from high position in the world to lowly service in the church. The story of this advancement is the story of a great struggle and a greater victory.

This servant and poet of the church, George Herbert, had won distinctions in early youth because of his great abilities and excellent conduct. Having been carefully taught by his pious mother and a family chaplain, at the age of twelve years he entered Westminster School, where he manifested studious habits and religious inclinations and became proficient in classical languages. After three years at Westminster he was elected to a scholarship at Trinity College, Cambridge.

Herbert was the type of a student from whom teachers expect great things. In addition to superior mental endowments, exemplary conduct, and religious convictions, he possessed enthusiasm and high ambitions, even to the extent that upon leaving Westminster the headmaster advised him to study moderately and to take physical exercise in order to preserve his health. At Cambridge University, the head of Trinity College admired the attractive and aristocratic young scholar, but, as has been suggested, may have felt that he kept himself at too great distance from his inferiors and showed too high an evaluation of himself and parentage.

During his career at Cambridge he attained the highest distinction possible for any student. He entered as a scholarship student, took the B.A. degree, and was elected first a minor, then a major fellow, received the M.A. degree, became a lecturer in the School of Rhetoric, and was elected to the highest office of the university, that of public orator, which office he held eight years.

This latter position was one not easily obtained and brought its possessor into contact with the great men of the day. The university orator was the official mouth-piece. His purpose was to secure the good will of influential persons by paying them compliments when they visited the university, to write letters for obtaining privileges, to express thanks for gifts and services rendered, and to send congratulations to other universities. Native or foreign princes were welcomed with an elaborate Latin speech. The orator was required to wear a gown of prescribed pattern and had a separate place of honor in public proceedings.

While seeking the oratorship, the conflict was going on in the life of George Herbert. He had been a youth of tender conscience and of a religious bent, had resolved to consecrate his abilities in poetry to God's glory, and had undertaken the study of divinity in preparation for service in the church. Some felt that the desire for the oratorship would detract too much from divinity studies and that the position had too many worldly connections, but Herbert himself thought "that this dignity hath no such earthiness in it but it may very well be joined with heaven." By soliciting the influence of relatives and friends, he succeeded in winning the election; and by means of elegance in speech and writing, ready wit and superior learning, he was able to fill the position with distinction.

The academic distinction thus attained fostered an ambition for places higher than that of university orator. Some of his predecessors had become Secretary of State. In order to obtain similar advancement, Herbert mastered Italian, Spanish, and French. He welcomed distinguished foreign diplomatists to the university with high and flowery compliments, and King James in such a gratulatory manner that he grew into the King's favor. Notable personages who accompanied the King were attracted by Herbert, and he soon came to be loved by the most eminent and powerful of the court nobility. His orations were "weighted with earthliness"; the outward glory of the world was becoming more attractive; the purpose of taking sacred orders in the church was more and more abandoned.

Such ambitions were not unnatural. For generations, the Herberts had been people of character and ability and servants of their country. All the six brothers of George Herbert were "brought up in learning"; all were famous duelists; and nearly all were in public life. One had been ambassador to France. But if desire for the life of a courtier was in line with paternal traditions, it was not in harmony with the wishes of his mother nor with his own previous plans. Herbert's attitude toward holding high office in the government was undoubtedly similar to his attitude toward the position of university orator—that there was "no such earthiness in it but it may very well be joined with heaven." Consequently he frequented court circles more assiduously, delegated his duties as orator to a deputy whenever the King was near Cambridge on hunting expeditions, and sought thus to forward his opportunities for promotion.

Suddenly and before any significant appointment was realized, his hopes were shattered. Two of his most influential court friends died and shortly thereafter, King James himself. Thereupon Herbert retired to the country home of a friend and reflected upon the future course of his life, whether to proceed with his aspiration for political standing, which was now more difficult to obtain, or whether to return to the former resolution of taking orders.

Many were the conflicts he passed through at the country home of his friend. It seemed that God had ended the lives of his powerful friends for a purpose, that he was called to higher things, that it had been divinely planned that he should be a "pattern of virtue to all posterity." He knew that he had a mission in life, and it was becoming more apparent that he was on the wrong road. The struggle was intense, because as his biographer, Izaac Walton, said, "Ambitious desires and the outward glory of this world are not easily laid aside." At the court were artifice, intrigue, bribe-taking, murder, divorce, and such corruptions; he was also afflicted with physical ailments premonishing a short life on earth. At an earlier age he had considered divinity the main business of his life and had resolved to devote his poetical powers to religious ends. He possessed the gifts of a courtier and the graces of a scholar and could have won a high place at court, but through conflict and anguish and tears and the transforming grace of God, he conquered his pride and high estimate of self and acquired true humility and a sense of unworthiness. He returned to London and told a friend that he planned to enter sacred orders. The friend tried to persuade Herbert to change his decision, as it was "too mean an employment, and too much below his birth and the excellent abilities and endowments of his mind." Herbert replied:

"It hath been formerly adjudged that the domestic servants of the King of heaven should be of the noblest families on earth; and though the iniquity of the late times have made clergymen meanly valued, and the sacred name of priest contemptible, yet I will labor to make it honorable by consecrating all my learning, and all my poor abilities, to advance the glory of that God that gave them; knowing that I can never do too much for Him that hath done so much for me as to make me a Christian. And I will labor to be like my Savior, by making humility lovely in the eyes of all men, and by following the merciful and meek example of my dear Jesus."

When George Herbert submitted himself to the supreme Will, he renounced the "gilded toys" of the world. He resumed the study of divinity, transformed a neglected, decayed, and fallen sanctuary of which he had been made prebend into a beautiful house of worship, and five years after the death of the King, the rectory of Fugglestone with Bemerton was bestowed upon him. Doubting his fitness for the responsible and holy work, he fasted, prayed, and meditated an entire month, but finally accepted it. The night after his induction he said to a friend:

"I now look back upon my aspiring thoughts, and think myself more happy than if I had attained what then I so ambitiously thirsted for: and I can now behold the court with an impartial eye, and see plainly that it is made up of fraud, and titles, and flattery, and many such empty, imaginary, painted pleasures that are so empty as not to satisfy when they are enjoyed. But in God and His service is a fulness of joy and pleasure, and no satiety. And I will now use all my endeavors to bring my relations and dependents to a love and reliance on Him who never fails those that trust Him. But above all I will be sure to live well, because the virtuous life of a clergyman is the most powerful eloquence to persuade all that see it to reverence and love, and at least to desire to live like Him. . . . And I beseech Him that my humble and charitable life may so win upon others as to bring glory to my Jesus, whom I have this day taken to be my Master and Governor: and I am so proud of His service that I will always observe, and obey, and do His will, and always call Him 'Jesus my Master'; and I will always condemn my birth, or any title or dignity that can be conferred upon me, when I shall compare them with my title of being a priest, and serving at the altar of Jesus, my Master."

Thus dedicating all natural advantages to the cause of Christ, he served humbly and whole-heartedly as a country parson and lived truly as a man of God. He had now forsaken all to follow Jesus. He repaired the decayed parts of the church building, helped and relieved the needy people of his parish, and instructed and guided them to a more zealous and reverential manner of public worship. Church prayers were held daily, and "some of the meaner sort of his parish did so love and reverence

Mr. Herbert that they would let their plough rest when Mr. Herbert's saints' bell rung to prayers, that they might also offer their devotions to God with him, and would then return back to plough."

After only three years of exhausting and self-sacrificing service, his saintly career was ended. He had found loyalty to the King of kings a greater loyalty than that to the king of England and had accepted the sphere of service wherein he could manifest the greater loyalty to Jesus, his Master.

Not only has George Herbert left a rare example of extraordinary consecration and fervent piety, but he has placed upon the altar of the church sweet and heavenly thoughts embodied in exquisite poetry picturing the many spiritual conflicts through which he passed before he consented to subject his will to that of Jesus, his Master. His reputation extends to our day chiefly because of his work as a writer of sacred poetry.

III

DILIGENCE REWARDED

HENRY WADSWORTH LONGFELLOW

THE board of trustees of Bowdoin College had a meeting that significantly affected the career of a certain young man. They voted to establish a department of modern languages at this then recently established institution. One of the trustees, Benjamin Orr, was a lover of Horace; while in service as an examiner at the senior examination, he had found a translation of an ode of Horace that showed excellent workmanship. The student who made the translation gave evidence of proficiency to the extent that Orr suggested him for the new position. The young man, Henry Wadsworth Longfellow, aged nineteen, and just graduating from college, was the fortunate appointee to the professorship.

The superiority of Longfellow's translation was not an accident. It represented habits and attitudes acquired by years of effort. He lived in a home of books and music, Sunday church attendance, Bible reading, childhood games, and school lessons. Already at six, the teacher said that he was one of the best boys in school, excelling both in studies and in conduct. He began writing poetry for publication when thirteen and entered Bowdoin as a student at fourteen. While there were various opportunities for outdoor diversions about the town, Longfellow preferred to devote himself to his studies and to efforts in poetical composition. He had left a comfortable home in Portland, Maine, for a cold, bleak room in Brunswick. His mother wrote expressing fear that learning might not flourish nor his ideas properly expand in a frosty atmosphere, in which case she would not receive the poetic effusions she expected from her son on New Year's Day. But the young man of slight, erect figure, delicate complexion, and intelligent expression of countenance progressed nevertheless in his studies and in his writings.

In a few years the young man's college career approached its end, and he faced the necessity of choosing a vocation. He felt that he did not have enough talent for argument to attain eminence as a lawyer, he did not consider himself good enough to be a minister, and he was not interested in medicine. He knew well enough what he wanted to be—a man of letters—but he also knew that his father, a lawyer and legislator, would have little sympathy with such an ambition. He did, however, secure permission to spend a year in literary study at Harvard after graduation from Bowdoin. But now came the unexpected appointment to the professorship of modern languages at Bowdoin, which started him on the career of his choice.

In offering Longfellow the professorship, the understanding was that he should first visit Europe for further study of languages, particularly French, Spanish, Italian, and German. So Henry Wadsworth Longfellow, the youth who hoped to attain eminence in literature, made arrangements to sail alone to far-away Europe. A transatlantic trip in those steamshipless days was an exceptional adventure and especially so for a boy of nineteen. But Henry was enthusiastic, and, after being provided with letters of introduction for presentation to European scholars, and after eight months of anxious waiting, he entered upon a thirty-day sailing journey and looked upon America for the last time in three years.

Those three years were years of exacting labor, for the mastery of languages is no after-dinner diversion. Furthermore, the financial allowance from his father was only six hundred dollars a year. He had been able to maintain high standing as a student in Portland and Brunswick, but now in France he began to realize his scholastic and intellectual limitations. He wrote to his father: "There are allurements enough around me, it is true, but I do not feel myself at liberty to indulge in them; and there is splendor enough, but it is a splendor in which I have no share. No! The truth is that the heavy responsibilities which I have taken upon myself, the disappointments I have met with in not finding my advantages so great as I had fancied them, and in finding my progress comparatively slow, together with the continual solicitude about the final results of my studies and the fear that you will be displeased with my expense, are hanging with a terrible weight upon me."

Thus with much drudgery, intermingled with some pleasure, Longfellow worked on month after month. He was not so well pleased with France, but found Spain charming. The language of each country was studied as he went. After having acquired a fair degree of mastery over French and Spanish, he proceeded to Italy, the land of his dreams. There he conquered Italian, and after a time was ready to grapple with German. He was now twenty-two and had already invested three valuable years in the privations of foreign travel, in friendly associations, in diligent study, in periods of loneliness and despair, and in the apparent sacrifice of a poetic career. While in Germany he received a letter from his parents asking him to come home because his sister was very ill and also because they thought he had been gone long enough. He decided to return at once, but his sister died by the time he reached Paris.

Four years after leaving Bowdoin, Longfellow entered the college as language professor. This position was his first major reward for diligence. Hard work was still a necessity, for it was his task to build up a new department of which he was now the head. He had to construct a curriculum, prepare grammars and readers to serve as textbooks for his students, prepare lectures, make translations, and act as librarian. All this work was done with vigor and thoroughness.

Eventually Professor Ticknor of Harvard made known his intention of resigning from his position as Smith Professor of Modern Languages. Who would be able to fill Ticknor's place better than Henry Wadsworth Longfellow? Due to various limitations at Bowdoin, Longfellow had been wanting a change for several years. Soon a letter came to the fortunate scholar offering him the Harvard position. He had reason to consider himself a lucky person in being offered such a place without making an effort to obtain it. After another period of time abroad he assumed the Harvard professorship, which he held during the next eighteen years.

To a greater extent than in teaching, his diligence was rewarded in literary accomplishments. Never idle, and always giving his best he devoted a long life to one calling, poetry. " 'Evangeline,' the flower of American idyls, known in all lands," was composed after careful study of the chronicles of Nova Scotia; its writing required diligent application because of its unfamiliar meter. " 'Evangeline' is so easy for you to read, because it was so hard for me to write," he said. As his lyrics and ballads had become popular favorites, so this classic tale immediately received a similar reception. In the department of translation Longfellow rendered a superior service. The translation of Dante's "Divine Comedy," which occupies three volumes of his works, required years of painstaking effort. Day after day before breakfast he added a number of lines until eventually the world was enriched with a version praised by scholars for its literal and natural diction.

The career of Henry Wadsworth Longfellow teaches what can be accomplished by diligent application to one's work. Though he had not great depth of powerful thought and emotion, he wrote poetry of such exquisite beauty and universal truth that he was for a time the most widely read poet of the English language. In addition to professorial position and literary fame he was rewarded with an attractive personality, love and honor, many kind friends, pleasant home life, and the privilege of having made a real contribution to American culture.

IV

IDEAL FRIENDSHIP

JOHN MILTON

FEW young men have had higher standards in goodness, beauty, and truth for life and art than John
Milton. He considered a virtuous life necessary for enduring work in poetry, and likewise for true friendship
which he regarded as one of the noble and sacred things
in human experience. To him friendship demanded
superiority of soul more than superiority of intellect. It
was more dependent on qualities of character than on
the writing of letters. It had a sincerity and sacredness
that was enduring, and placed the individual received as
a friend above suspicion. It was fostered by a loving
recollection of virtues on both sides. Advancement in
friendship was impossible with anyone who lacked the
ingredients of moral excellence.

In addition to such high standards, there were evi-
dently qualities in Milton's personality that further
limited the number of his friends. In youth he had a
conviction of future greatness and a feeling of superiority and self-sufficiency that tended toward egotism. In
controversy he believed himself in the right and was
little disposed to accept the ideas of his contemporaries.
Consequently, intellectual independence barred him from
association with the thinking men of his time. Contact
with great minds through study was preferable to personal association with contemporaries in clubs or organ-
izations. In youth he withdrew from society for pur-

poses of study; in middle life his political and religious views made him unpopular; and later blindness necessitated a retreat from social activities.

Milton had, however, qualities that made him a very desirable friend. Although he took life seriously, he was sufficiently affable to be a pleasant companion. His ability and learning brought him many admiring visitors whom he cheerfully and courteously received. Henry Lawes wanted verses to set to music. Samuel Hartlib came for ideas on education. Thomas Ellwood came for assistance in Latin; Dryden to get permission to transform "Paradise Lost" into an opera; Roger Williams to discuss the subject of liberty; and sons of leading Englishmen came to be taught. The politeness of the host lessened the difficulty of approach in case any caller felt ill at ease in the presence of the scholar and poet.

A friendship with Milton was slowly formed and seldom broken. His integrity was unchanging, and he did not betray his friends nor use them as tools. He calls the Deity to witness that he never once deviated from the paths of uprightness, for he knew that though his conduct "might escape the notice of men, it could not elude the inspection of God." He affirmed that he never sought positions of honor through the medium of friends. To be a friend of John Milton was truly a privilege, for in spite of his limitations in experience and disposition, he possessed the essential and most valuable qualities of a true friend.

On one occasion during those years when the studious young poet was withdrawing from society at Cambridge for purposes of study and retiring for literary leisure through summer vacations, he received in a Greek letter a cheering message from a friend who fully measured up to the highest ideals of friendship:

"But thou, wonder that thou art, why dost thou despise the gifts of nature? Why dost thou persist inexcusably in hanging all night and all day over books and literary exercises? Live, laugh, enjoy youth, and the hours as they pass, and desist from those researches of yours into the pursuits, and leisures, and indolences of the wise men of old, yourself a martyr to overwork all the while."

Persistent application to intellectual pursuits had deprived Milton of many of the pleasures of young people. School friends were not many, but while at St. Paul's School in London a friendship was formed that became the most excellent of all. This young friend, the writer of the Greek letter, was a gay young Italian, Charles Diodati, who ever wrote so frankly and delightfully to the serious poet. Diodati was a member of a distinguished Italian family. After completion of the course at St. Paul's, Milton entered Cambridge and Diodati Oxford, but the friendship was continued by correspondence and vacation excursions.

No friend could mean as much to Milton as did Diodati. Others had made worthy contributions, but the poet needed someone in those early years to whom he could unreservedly reveal his inner life with the assurance of being understood, someone who could aid in his social development. He did not need to be stimulated to harder study but needed rather a sympathetic appreciation of his work. This appreciation he abundantly received, for none was so ready with praise as this sprightly Italian.

The correspondence of these two friends is a rich expression of mutual loyalty and devotion and of noble ideals of friendship. In another Greek letter, Diodati reminded Milton of an excursion they had planned to take. On account of stormy and unsettled weather, Diodati was afraid his grave comrade would decide not to go, so he wrote to encourage him, to put him into a joyous frame of mind, and to tell how he longed for his society. "So much do I long for your society that in my longing I am dreaming and all but prophesying fine weather, and calm, and all things golden, for tomorrow, that we may regale ourselves mutually with philisophical and learned discourses."

A message so breezy and full of sunshine was surely not disregarded. It rather inspired Milton to express a similar and equally sincere eagerness for the society of his friend. He hoped God would never permit him to become a traitor to friendship, and he really considered it impossible not to love men like Diodati. He saw in the character of this genial friend the image of supreme beauty. In statements addressed to him, Milton said that if he had met a man who dared to feel and speak and be what the highest wisdom had taught to be best, and had failed to attach himself to him in friendship, he would have felt that he missed an opportunity for the enrichment of his life. Such outer circumstances as wealth, rank, profession, intellect, or party would not be the deciding factors; it was rather the inner spirit of the man that determined the extent to which he reached Milton's standard.

Having completed his student career at Cambridge and studied quietly for six years in his father's house at Horton, Milton made a continental tour with special attention to Italy. His keen interest in things Italian and particularly the language was an outgrowth of this great friendship of his youth. While on this tour, he composed a number of Italian sonnets and addressed one to Diodati. But a sad thing had happened in England. The friend whom he thought was living and to whom he had addressed a sonnet had passed away. The poet, now in Florence, had left England and Diodati a little more than four months before; at the time of the death of his friend, he often thought of him and naturally talked about him to his new Florentine acquaintances, little thinking that he was never to see him again.

When Milton, after returning to England, visited his old neighbors and friends, it was with sad reflections that he realized his great loss. The thoughts of grief and mourning were eventually given permanent form in a Latin pastoral elegy containing the repeated line, "Go unpastured, my lambs, your master now heeds not your bleating."

With human freedom now at stake in England, the poet devoted all his resources to the great struggle, became with Cromwell a leader of the Commonwealth, and wrote his vigorous prose denunciations. After the Restoration, he produced his magnificent epics. But the memory of Charles Diodati never left him. What this friend of his young manhood did in enriching the life of John Milton none other could have done.

V

THE CHARM OF OLD THINGS

WASHINGTON IRVING

IN a quaint, old-fashioned structure, built according to Dutch style, and in one of the oldest cities of America, New York, lived a little boy in a home where all the brothers and sisters were older than himself. Soon he began to wander through the streets of the town, past the old-style houses, down to the wharves and out on the piers. There he watched the sail boats and dreamed about sailing the wide ocean some day. Sometimes in mischievous mood he clambered over the roofs of city houses and dropped stones down the chimneys. His father, a deacon and very strict, did not even want his children to read stories of adventure, but Washington, not always obedient, did so nevertheless. Apparently he was also something of an idler, for he never received much schooling. But everyone knew after all that this tender-hearted, loving, dreaming youngster, Washington Irving, was not altogether a nuisance.

He loved adventure. When fifteen he explored the Sleepy Hollow region and thereafter made frequent excursions up the Hudson and Mohawk Rivers into the wild lands of New York. He lived on a new continent, in a new nation where new principles of government and high ideals of religion were to have free growth. "Go west, young man" was the slogan, but somehow the soul of Washington Irving heard and responded to some quiet voices of the past and the old and was not greatly aroused by the trumpet call of the present and the new. It soon became his fortune to go east instead of west, to wander in the Old World instead of in the new.

In his delicate body, consumptive tendencies began to develop, and to save his life his brothers put their money together and sent him to Europe. "There's a chap who will go overboard before we get across," said the captain to himself, but he was mistaken. Irving strolled about the towns and country of France, mingled in delightful society in Italy, and explored the ruins of Sicily, all the while imbibing the spirit of the old world. The great American west never touched his earlier life; it was the associations of an old civilization that stimulated him to a successful career. But even yet he was not certain about a vocation.

After returning to America, he finally found a rich storehouse at his door. From childhood he had peered into the Dutch background of New York, and with strong attraction for the old soon felt its charm. He now looked afresh into the "good old Dutch times," into an antiquity of his native city which extended to "the regions of doubt and fable." From those regions he dug out enough material to produce the first masterpiece of American humor, *Diedrich Knickerbocker's History of New York.* He had considered the period of Dutch domination the poetic age of his city, and now in an amusing form he embodied its traditions and illustrated its customs.

A few years later Irving joined his brothers, Peter and Ebenezer, as merchants and importers of hardware. In the interests of the company he was sent to Washington, where he devoted his time to society and amusements. Afterward he visited his brother Peter in Liverpool, where the business needed more attention than the indolent young man of pleasure liked to give it. Things became more embarrassing and finally the business sunk into bankruptcy. With high regard Washington's brothers had hitherto rendered him much assistance; in turn he now became the mainstay of the family. He went to London, threw himself into literary work, and shared his earnings with his unfortunate brothers.

London! What a paradise for the lover of the picturesque, the romantic, the old! Exploration of London was adventure after Irving's own heart. He found a section called Little Britain, a small neighborhood with "very venerable and debilitated houses" where in ancient times the Dukes of Brittany had their lordly family mansions. There he lived quietly in one of the smallest but oldest edifices, which was equipped with old furniture. He enjoyed the antiquated folks and fashions, the ancient holiday games and customs of Little Britain.

In a half-dreaming mood he loitered about the old gray cloisters of Westminster Abbey. He deciphered nearly obliterated tombstone inscriptions; stepped softly among the sepulchers of dead kings, the tombs of warriors, courtiers, and statesmen, and meditated on the thoughts of former sages, the chivalry of knights, and battles of long ago. He entered a lofty antique hall, the library of Westminster, where an ancient picture of some church dignitary hung over the fireplace, and where in moldering covers old volumes were ranged on the shelves. "A ramble through the Abbey," said Irving, "seemed like stepping back into the regions of antiquity, and losing myself among the shades of former ages."

The relics of old times were the objects of his silent searchings. On a summer ramble, after pushing through a bustling throng, he entered a quiet, obscure lane and came upon the Chapel of the Knights Templar, a very ancient chapel with ancient tombs. Upon another occasion he wandered through the dull streets until he came to "a Gothic gateway of mouldering antiquity." Here was an old edifice, Charter House, in which age had overtaken everything he saw and nearly everybody he met.

Old houses, churches, castles, inns, ever attracted. Rip Van Winkle, the hero in that famous story bearing the same name, had a time-worn and weather-beaten house. The residence of Baron Von Landshort in *The Specter Bridegroom* was an old castle, and in *The Student of Salamanca* the alchemist lived in a ruined fragment, an old tower which was part of an old castle. In *The Tales of a Traveler* a fox-hunting old Baronet kept bachelor's hall in "an ancient rook-haunted family mansion"; in an ancient chateau an adventurous uncle retired for the night in an extremely old tower where he heard the old clock strike the midnight hour and then met in his room the spirit of one departed; the aunt resided in an old country-seat; Grandfather rode up to an old rickety inn; and an antiquary, a collector of old coins, always groped among ruins. Bracebridge Hall, where Irving during a Christmas and again at a wedding was a guest, was a stronghold of old fashions and old English hospitality. The Squire, an old country gentleman, represented the oldest family in the neighborhood. He preferred authors of two centuries ago, wanted his children to play the old English games, and advocated the revival of old holiday observances. He praised the old style of traveling— horseback—and railed against the more modern stage-coaches, post chaises, and turnpike roads. The house-keeping was in the old English style, meals consisted of genuine old fare; old family portraits and relics were preserved. What a glorious time Irving must have had at Bracebridge Hall!

Irving always admired old customs. Ancient funeral and holiday customs exercised a delightful spell over his imagination. He thought that the faint, lingering vestiges of ancient customs imparted a charm to rustic life and softened the rudeness of rustic manners.

"Newstead Abbey," he wrote, "is one of the finest specimens in existence of those quaint and romantic piles, half castle, half convent, which remain as monuments of the olden times of England." In this monastery-palace, the ancestral mansion of Byron, Irving for three weeks inhabited a magnificent suite of rooms, richly decorated, and containing antique dignified furniture and curious old relics. He strolled about the old Abbey gardens, passed along the ancient stone walls, and viewed the ancient statues. A sojourn in this mysterious- looking mansion, haunted by monkish and feudal associations, was a delightful experience.

Then also the seventeen-year stay in Europe included Spain, the land of romance and legend and ruins, of glory and color and charm. His home was the Alhambra, "a royal palace and warrior castle," the former residence of Moorish kings and Castilian monarchs, "laid out with courts and gardens, fountains and baths, and stately halls." He was quartered in one of the remote and ruined apartments, surrounded by secluded gardens containing fountains sparkling among roses and myrtles, with orange and citron trees near by. In this enchanted castle he wandered through empty halls and mysterious chambers; their peculiar charm called up "vague reveries and picturings of the past." Through many quiet hours he

sat in the Jesuit's Library relishing old Spanish chronicles and gleaning facts concerning historical characters.

Thus Irving spent many years enriching his mind with
the glory of old things, and refining his spirit with their
charm. His wanderings led him to many ancient relics,
but he somehow missed the charm of the greatest, "The
Old Rugged Cross." His latest biographer refers to the
absence of religious motivation in his life, to his lack of
Christian faith. The reader of his works finds few references to "The Old, Old Story." The old abiding Faith,
the old inspired Book, and the old rugged Cross—what
an attraction those old relics and present all-potent
realities contain and are! How can one afford to miss
them!

VI

DEEP IN HUMILITY

JOHN WOOLMAN

A READER of the journal wherein John Woolman recorded his experiences of the goodness of God will readily perceive that its author entered farther and deeper into humility than people ordinarily choose to do. He will observe how this pious Friend found a wonderful peace and happiness by following the vision and the desire he thus expressed: "Through the revelation of Jesus Christ, I had seen the happiness of humility, and there was an earnest desire in me to enter deep into it, and at times this desire arose to a degree of fervent supplication."

Although John Woolman did not make the full and complete consecration of his life to God until his twenty-first year, his sensitive spirit had early responded to the sweet influences of the Christian religion. By church attendance and by reading the Holy Scriptures and other religious books and also by the pious instructions of parents, he had early become acquainted with the operations of divine love. When other boys used ill language he was troubled and by the mercy of God was preserved from it. Having made at the age of twelve an undutiful reply to his mother who had reproved him for some misconduct, he was advised by his father to be more careful in the future. This awakened him to a sense of his wickedness; he retired and prayed to the Lord to forgive him and ever after that spoke respectfully to his parents.

After the age of sixteen, by acquiring new acquaintances and neglecting to read the Holy Scriptures, he came to find delight in youthful vanities. Through an illness, however, he was brought to a deep sense of folly and was humbled before God. Later he lost ground and again found pleasure in youthful mirth and vanity. At the age of eighteen, however, through sore conflicts, he felt the judgments of God in his soul like a consuming fire, and eventually was made, he says, to bow down before the Most High.

"I remember one evening I had spent some time in reading a pious author, and walking out alone, I humbly prayed to the Lord for His help, that I might be delivered from those vanities which so ensnared me. Thus being brought low He helped me, and as I learned to bear the cross, I felt refreshment to come from His presence; but not keeping in that strength which gave victory I lost ground again, the sense of which greatly afflicted me and I sought deserts and lonely places, and there with tears did confess my sins to God, and humbly craved help of Him, and I may say with reverence He was near to me in my troubles, and in those times of humiliation opened my ear to discipline."

As he now lived under the cross, his mind became more enlightened, his heart was made tender and contrite, and a universal love to his fellow creatures increased in him. He now kept from improper company, attended church services regularly, and spent Sunday afternoons reading the Scriptures and other good books.

Until the age of twenty-one, Woolman lived with his parents and worked on the plantation. At that age he became employed to tend the shop and keep books for a man whose business was shopkeeping and baking. As he left his father's house, he found his heavenly Father merciful to him beyond expression. He prayed that since his work would be of a more public nature, he would be enabled to serve God in humility and self-denial. With his life now fully dedicated to the Master's service, he began to speak a few words publicly in meeting and became a minister, in which calling he served the remainder of his life. More clearly he became convinced that to place his whole trust in God was best for him; consequently he abandoned all desire for outward greatness and fully chose the plain and simple life.

"I saw that an humble man, with the blessing of the Lord, might live on a little, and that where the heart was set on greatness, success in business did not satisfy the craving; but that commonly with an increase of wealth, the desire for wealth increased. There was a care on my mind so to pass my time, as to things outward, that nothing might hinder me from the most steady attention to the voice of the true Shepherd."

The employer of Woolman also employed a tailor, and Woolman came to believe that this would be a suitable trade for him. He felt that as a tailor he could get a living in a plain way without being encumbered with much business, and he further believed that the hand of Providence pointed out this employment to him and taught him to be content in it, even though he was at times disposed to seek something greater. As years passed the possibility for large business appeared, but having learned to be content with a plain way of living, he felt he should avoid cumbering affairs. In perplexity, he prayed to God, Who graciously heard him and gave him a heart resigned to His holy will. He limited himself to his trade as a tailor, without the help of an assistant, and ceased selling merchandise. He was still a busy man, for he was now engaged in some farming and was a surveyor and conveyancer. He was also an expert nurseryman and for a number of years was a teacher during intervals of his travels.

During the thirty years following his entrance into the ministry, John Woolman made many journeys throughout the eastern provinces, chiefly to preach and to visit friends who had slaves. Often with one companion or more, but sometimes alone, he journeyed in performance of the task to which he believed himself called—the liberation of the enslaved Negro. Sometimes he found it difficult to speak about the release of slaves, but he did his work in the spirit of love and depended on God for assistance. "I do not repine at having so unpleasant a task assigned me, but look with awfulness to Him Who appoints to His servants their respective employments and is good to all."

Having learned in his travels to be faithful to the Lord and content with His will, he experienced the heavenly blessing on his labors. All his work was performed in the spirit of humility, and all his experiences made him humble. On one page of his Journal are these expressions: "I had cause humbly to adore Him," "was made humbly thankful to the Lord," and "went home under a humbling sense of the gracious dealings of the Lord with me." Of one journey he said, "our gracious Father preserved us in a humble dependence on Him through deep exercises that were mortifying to the creaturely will." Of another he wrote, "For the favors and protection of the Lord, both inward and outward, in this little journey my heart is humbled in grateful acknowledgements." On other occasions he referred to the humbling power of

truth, the humbling goodness of the Lord, and the soften-
ing of the heart into humble contrition. He believed that
his public labors helped to keep him humble, that humility opened doors to divine wisdom and truth, that his
mind was humbled under the power of divine love, that
by humble meditation on the perfections of God we shall
understand His language, and that the humility of Jesus
Christ is a pattern for us to walk by.

In many ways Woolman's deep humility was manifested. During the last five years of his life all his distant travels were on foot. He believed that thus the
Lord called him to travel "that by so traveling I might
have a more lively feeling of the condition of the
oppressed slaves, set an example of lowliness before the
eyes of their masters, and be more out of the way of
temptation to unprofitable familiarities, and be less
expense amongst them."

Against luxury, especially too costly wearing apparel,
he ever gave testimony. He urged parents to educate
their children in true humility and the disuse of all
superfluities, and taught that a plain and simple way of
living would assure more peace and calmness of mind.
Dyed garments in his later years came to be considered
objectionable, but the singularity occasioned by wearing
a hat the natural color of the fur was a trial to him. He
nevertheless trusted that the Lord would support him
in the trial of being different from his brethren, and also
felt an inward consolation in the belief that the wearing
of the undyed hat was not in his own will.

The humility of John Woolman expressed itself in a
special tenderness and love for the unfortunate and the
oppressed. The keynote of all his writings is love to
God and love to man, and it was love that motivated his

many years of labor in behalf of the Negro. His sincerity in this respect was involved in his frequent tasks of executing bills of sale and drawing wills. While still working under an employer he was directed to write a bill of sale for a Negro woman. He complied but was afflicted in mind and told his employer that he considered the practice of slavekeeping inconsistent with the Christian religion. After this his life was dedicated to the life-long effort to free the slave. A little later, when requested to write the will for a sick person who intended to leave his slaves to his children, after seeking the will of the Lord he found it necessary to refuse. Only in cases where freedom of the slaves was permitted did he consent to write wills. If on his journeys he was entertained freely by people who lived in ease on the hard toil of their slaves, he felt distressed; he was more contented where the masters helped bear the burden and were considerate of their slaves. Sometimes upon leaving a home where he had been entertained he left money for the slaves that he might be free from the gain of oppression. In his later years he did not feel that he could conscientiously use sugar because it was the product of slave labor. He believed the Negroes were human beings with souls and that for our conduct toward them we must answer before God.

The Indians were also objects of his love and concern, and he desired to spend some time with them that he might understand them better and be more sympathetic. A decision was made to journey to some tribes living two hundred miles from Philadelphia. Such a visit seemed very weighty, so he turned to the Lord for support that he might not fail of following Him wheresoever He might lead. In his observations he found that many white people often sell rum to the Indians, thereby depriving them of their reason and causing quarrels and bitterness to arise; also when intoxicated they sell at a low price for more rum the skins and furs they had gotten through much fatigue and hard travels in hunting. As he reflected on the restless mind of the Indian, and on wars and battles, miseries and distresses of their wounded warriors, the desire to cherish the spirit of love and peace among them arose very fresh in him. He held some meetings with them, spoke to them through interpreters, and prayed for them. "A near sympathy with them was raised in me, and my heart being enlarged in the love of Christ I thought that the affectionate care of a good man for his only brother in affliction does not exceed what I then felt for that people."

On his last and longest journey, his voyage to England, his heart was turned in love to the sailors, and in private conversations he labored to turn them to a fear of the Lord. The corrupt and profane life of sailors, and their difficulties during storms and rainy weather, impressed upon him the great dangers to which lads are exposed who go to sea to learn the art of sailing, and he had a sympathizing tenderness toward them.

By thus continually walking humbly before God, seeking His will in all things, loving God and man with the whole heart, living a life of purity, simplicity, and great self-denial, with a constant testimony against luxury, and following the example of Jesus in meekness under suffering, John Woolman was enabled to live a life that was particularly useful, happy, and God-honoring.

VII

THE CHARM OF COMMON THINGS

WILLIAM WORDSWORTH

BECAUSE "the world is too much with us," we waste our lives in satisfying material wants; consequently we are out of tune with God's created world and are not moved by the bare-bosomed sea, the howling winds, "and every common sight." At least this was the opinion of William Wordsworth, an English poet who clearly saw and charmingly revealed "the loveliness and wonders of the world before us"; a philosopher who preferred "plain living and high thinking" to material wealth and show; a teacher who taught youth "to see, to think, and to feel"; and a man to whom Nature had been "all in all" but who later heard "the still sad music of humanity."

An "exquisite regard for common things" gave the poet a deep joy, an abiding pleasure, and an unfailing gratitude for human life. There was no need to gaze at the far away and long ago, to search for wisdom in books and schools, to interview great men; for Wordsworth found worth and wisdom in lowly men, education through contact with natural objects and enlarged sympathies in the "common face of Nature."

Delight in common things was nurtured in the early days of youth. He was born and lived in Cumberland, England, a region of silent lakes and purple mountains. Along the terraced walk behind his father's house flowed the beauteous Derwent River, whose music told him of the calmness of Nature. When he wrote the "Prelude" he still remembered bathing at the age of five in a small rill of this river on a summer day, and how in early happy years he and his only sister, Dorothy, played childhood games in the large old-fashioned garden above the terraced walk. He remembered, too, that at the age of nine, alone on frosty autumnal nights, he wandered among the mountainous cliffs and hollows with moon and stars shining overhead; and in the spring over high and lonely mountain peaks he climbed to ransack ingloriously the raven's nest. There in half-inch fissures of the slippery rock he hung on naked crags.

From the village of Hawkshead, where he attended school, the lakes, woods, open fields, and craggy hills could be reached in a few moments. During spare hours of those school days he fished in "forlorn cascades," ranged the mountains, and occasionally visited ancient landmarks on horseback, or rowed races on Windermere.

As a young man Wordsworth resided for a time in France. It was the period of the French Revolution, a movement from which he expected great benefits for mankind but realized only disappointment. That experience not only brought awful scenes of blood and terror to the outward view but oppressed him inwardly with sorrow, vexing thoughts, confused opinions, and loss of hope. But after observing those "spectacles of woe," he was delighted anew when he beheld once more in England the common things of earth. He saw gentle breezes bend the "heads of lordly pines" and shift "stupendous clouds through the whole compass of the sky"; he heard the gently muttering brooks and the waves stealing forth "to kiss the pebbly shore." These harmonious voices revealed to him that though evil operates in the doings of man, spring and summer always return to give happiness.

How charming are trees upon a college campus! Often had Wordsworth as a student wandered in the silent evening on the walks and among the groves of Cambridge. The lofty elms gave composure to the neighborhood. Standing beneath an ash whose boughs were wreathed with trailing ivy, he looked up at the lonely tree and his mind was calmed with tranquil visions.

The historian who revives the events of departed years may claim respect. To Wordsworth the common butterfly was the historian of his infancy; he begged this "gay creature" to remain in his sight, for it brought to mind the pleasant days of childhood when he and his sister chased the butterfly. He rushed boldly after it, but she "feared to brush the dust from off its wings."

To gaze upon the distant stars and search them out over the infinite heavenly spaces affords delight and wonder. The discoverer of a new star wins praise and medals, but is Wordsworth not right when he considers himself as great as the sage astronomer since he found the flower, the little celandine? This glittering, pleasant-faced flower, says the poet, is a "prophet of delight and mirth," a forerunner of spring, and is satisfied with the meanest place — moor, wood, or lane. It is not "beyond the moon" but at our feet, and charms not only the poet but likewise "the dim-eyed curious bee."

The sweet daisy, "the poet's darling," often gave love, delight, and memory when he lay in the shade to escape the hot summer sunshine. This little flower, only an "unassuming commonplace of Nature," had little to do or see, yet it gave the poet gladness and a share of its meek nature. Though so ordinary, it possessed qualities that made him think of it as a demure nun, a sprightly maiden, a queen with a crown of rubies, a little Cyclops with one eye, and a pretty, glittering star.

"I love a public road; there are few sights that please me more." When in his walks of youth, the poet looked ahead and saw the road disappear in the hills, it seemed to him like a "guide into eternity." Even in the quietness and solitude of night he loved "to walk alone along the public way." The road offered views of common things and changing scenes; it provided time for meditation and an opportunity to meet fellow travelers. There he met "strolling bedlamites" and "uncouth vagrants." When he conversed with those he met,

> *The lonely roads*
> *Were schools to me in which I daily read*
> *With most delight the passions of mankind,*
> *There saw into the depths of human souls.*

In walks on lonely roads the poet found hope, peace, pleasure, healing, repose, and honorable words from lowly and obscure people. Among the many he met and wrote about were: a little cottage girl who to all his questions only answered, "We are seven"; an aged Cumberland beggar who sat beside the highway eating fragments of food given by the village dames, and who kept alive among the people the qualities of sympathy and charity; an old huntsman, Simon Lee, who tried in vain to loosen the root of a stump, but could not, and shed tears of gratitude when the poet with one blow did the task for him.

What would this world be without the sun? Wordsworth loved the sun because he had seen him lay "his beauty on the morning hills." All the beauty and loveliness of earth and "the sweetness of a common dawn" were possible because of an ordinary everyday sun that rules in unfailing splendor. And suppose there were no moon to reign as queen of the night! The moon was dear to the poet as he looked upon her "while she hung midway between the hills."

To William Wordsworth all common things of earth had a charm, a beauty, and a loveliness, and were capable of arousing joyous emotions. Summer nights, woods at noon, the margin of the trembling lake, leafless trees, icy crags, distant hills, solitary cliffs, the orange sky of evening, clear sparkling stars, fleecy clouds, mountain brooks, winter snows, curling mist, summer shade, midnight storm, rippling breezes, fresh flowers, cottage windows, budding twigs, wreaths of smoke, murmuring waters, sounding cataracts, the living air, the blue sky, green meadows, misty mountain winds, the sparkling foam, the shady nook of hazels, moss-fleeced stones, a spreading oak, lordly pines, the warbling skylark, the green linnet, the melodious birds, a simple child, the glad face of a sweet highland girl, golden daffodils, the cheerful daisy, the mountain echo, a frosty morn, flowery lawns, shepherds, and bridges — these and many other ordinary things have been the subjects of his meditations. It is a cheerful faith to believe that "all which we behold is full of blessings." To the seeing eye and hearing ear a "mighty sum of things forever speaks."

Is anything more common than a brother or a sister, and has ever a poet had a more valued and devoted sister than William Wordsworth? Dorothy Wordsworth in her letters to a friend referred to her brother's superior qualities, his affection for her, and her great regard for him. "He was never afraid of comforting his sister; he never left her in anger; he always met her with joy; he preferred her society to every other pleasure." The Wordsworth children were orphans, having early lost Father and Mother and home, and William and Dorothy were in youth separated for long periods of time. In one letter William wrote to her: "Oh, my dear, dear sister, with what transport shall I again meet you! with what rapture shall I again wear out the day in your sight? . . . I see you in a moment running, or rather flying to my arms."

It was the poet's sister who dispelled his gloom after the dark days of the French Revolution. She had confidence in his character and poetic abilities, persuaded him that he was born to be a poet, devoted herself to his improvement, and dedicated her life to his life and work. Together they traveled through the Lake district of England, to Germany, to Scotland. After receiving a legacy from a friend they were able to maintain a home of their own. They settled first at Racedown Lodge, Dorsetshire, then near Coleridge at Alfoxden, Somersetshire, and later at Grasmere in the lake district of northern England near the place of their birth. In this lake and mountain region "of unsurpassed beauty and loveliness," they lived in a small house, Dove Cottage, which overlooked the beauteous lake of Grasmere. It was, said DeQuincy, "a little white cottage, gleaming in the midst of trees, with a vast and seemingly never-ending series of accents rising above it, to the height of more than three thousand feet." Behind the house, in a small garden and orchard, sparkled a spring of pure water amidst apple trees and primroses and daffodils.

There in seclusion the poet and his sister planted trees and flowers and took daily walks together. She read to him, transcribed his poems, and with her quick eye helped him find the mystery and beauty of Nature. William was naturally stern and harsh, but Dorothy's sweetness and gentleness softened his severe countenance. He thanked her in his poetry for her "early tenderness" and wrote, "But thou didst soften down this oversternness." Although he later married Mary Hutchinson, Dorothy ever remained his close companion and comforter, "the lady who paced by his side continually through sylvan and mountain tracts," the sharer of his delight in natural objects.

"The world is too much with us." In and above the grandeur of nature shines the glory of God. One may obtain help from the solid hills but beyond the hills is the Almighty Creator, the only reliable source of joy and comfort and blessing. The pleasures at the right hand of God are more abiding than the delights of this beautiful earth. The mysteries of the divine surpass the mysteries of the ordinary. It is well to enjoy with Wordsworth the blessings of the common things of earth, but may no one forget that from heaven comes man's greatest happiness and good.

William Wordsworth was brought up in the Church of England and was a high churchman. He was familiar with the Bible, the Prayer Book, and the devotional writings of the great Anglican divines. He thought that the safest training for the mind in religion was in contemplating the character and personal history of Christ. His early poetry has often been considered pantheistic, but this is denied by some scholars. It is said that he knew the Christian doctrine that God reveals Himself through and is present in nature and is more than nature.

There were, however, some points of the Christian creed he had difficulty in believing, and he was unaffected by the evangelical movement of his day. A recent scholarly work by Edith Batho contains the following statement: "It was evangelical theology which emphasized particularly the extreme sinfulness and degradation of man and the atonement through the death of Christ; and that Wordsworth, even when writing on religious themes, should have very little to say about either, nothing about hell, and on the contrary a great deal to say about the divine in man, shocked many religious people."

We are not to judge his creed from the fewness of the Christian references in his poetry, for he himself said: "I have been averse to frequent mention of the mysteries of Christian faith," but he also declared his disbelief in eternal punishment and in human depravity and can therefore not be considered in harmony with Biblical and orthodox Christianity.

VIII

LIVING IN THE WOODS

HENRY DAVID THOREAU

"THERE is a pleasure in the pathless woods." The pioneer settlers loved to tell their experiences in clearing the forests, building rude houses, and hearing through the stormy night the roar of giant trees and the wild howl of wolves and panthers. We, their descendants, enjoy listening to the stories and sometimes wish that for a short time we might have their experiences in reality as well as in imagination. Still real to our own lives is the sight of the shady woods as we pass them on hot summer days. We enter their cool atmosphere, walk through the solemn temples, and would gladly linger longer there; but how seldom we make our fancies real!

The summer cottage by the wooded lake has become a common thing, so common in fact that the seclusion and solitude of the woods are gone; the artificialities of civilized life are too prevalent; and the novelty and value of the whole experience is much minimized. Henry David Thoreau put the thought into action, and he did it in such a primitive fashion that he was able to extract the whole flavor of out-door life. He actually did build a cabin in the woods and lived there away from civilization, more than two years.

Who was Thoreau, and why did he live in the woods? He was a man who has come to be considered one of the most original of American writers. In his own day he was misjudged and ignored for few understood him. He was born in Concord, Massachusetts, then a town of about two thousand inhabitants. After attending local schools, he entered Harvard at the age of sixteen. He was more interested in the library than in routine class-room work or in teachers. A fellow student in describing him said that Thoreau was cold and lived apart from his class mates. In earlier boyhood, in addition to doing the family chores, he roamed much about the woods and meadows. Concerning his college life, he wrote to the secretary of his class: "Though bodily I have been a member of Harvard University, heart and soul I have been far away among the scenes of my boyhood. Those hours that should have been devoted to study have been spent in scouring the woods and exploring the lakes and streams of my native village. Immured within the dark but classic walls of a Stoughton or a Hollis, my spirit yearned for the sympathy of my old and almost forgotten friend, Nature."

It is evident then that Thoreau's forest life was not lived because he was an Indian, a rail-splitter, or a pioneer frontier settler. He was none of these, but he has had other appellations. He has been called a gypsy-scholar, a poet-naturalist, a bachelor of nature, and a cosmic Yankee. He himself wrote, "I am a mystic, a transcendentalist, and a natural philosopher."

While still in school, he began to collect Indian relics. He was expert in finding them, and once when out walking with a friend was asked where Indian arrowheads could be found. "Everywhere," he replied, and picked one up instantly.

Leaving Harvard, Thoreau began to teach in his home town. He loved children and understood their ways of thinking. He retold for them classical myths and Indian legends and took them with him in many of his country rambles. His methods of discipline were interfered with, so after three years of teaching, he turned to other employments.

"The art of living well" was one aim of Henry David Thoreau. He refused to enter a profession that would destroy his personal freedom. For a time he experimented in the occupation of his father, the manufacture of lead pencils. He succeeded in making one equal to the best and then made no more. The endless walks and studies of natural history were continued. His skill in mensuration and his familiarity with the Concord region enabled him to become an excellent surveyor. When he needed money he earned it by surveying, planting, building a boat or fence, and numerous other manual tasks. Ten years after graduation from Harvard, official inquiries were made regarding the situations of the graduates of his class. Thoreau wrote: "I don't know whether mine is a profession, or a trade, or what not. It is not yet learned, and in every instance has been practiced before being studied. It is not one, but legion. I will give you some of the monsters' heads. I am a schoolmaster, a private tutor, a surveyor, a gardener, a farmer, a painter (I mean a house painter), a carpenter, a mason, a day laborer, a pencil-maker, a glass-paper-maker, a writer, and sometimes a poetaster."

Not only did Thoreau continually study the rivers and ponds, fishes, birds, trees, and all plants and animals of his Concord environment, but he made frequent brief excursions to other regions. While a teacher, he spent a week of his vacation on a voyage of exploration on the Concord and Merrimac Rivers. He took three trips to the Maine woods, traveled in Montreal and Quebec, and made many short tours in his native State. He was a skillful camper, walking usually on his trips, carrying a few articles tied in a handkerchief or piece of brown paper and spending the night out-of-doors, in a farmhouse or a fisherman's cabin.

At the age of twenty-eight, Thoreau borrowed an axe, walked south of Concord one and one-half miles into the pine woods beside Walden Pond, and began to cut down the tall white pines in order to build a house. This labor was continued until several months later, when the house was completed at a total cost of twenty-eight dollars and twelve and one-half cents. It consisted of one room ten feet wide and fifteen feet long that served as kitchen, bedroom, and parlor combined. For furniture there were a bed, a table, a desk, three chairs, a looking glass three inches in diameter, and such household utensils as a kettle, skillet, frying-pan, dipper, wash bowl, knives, forks, plates, one cup and one spoon.

A two and one-half acre tract of light sandy, virgin soil was plowed and cultivated for the production of vegetables. Thoreau planted beans chiefly, but also some potatoes, corn, peas, and turnips, and was able to reduce his expenses for food to eight dollars and seventy-four cents for an eight months' period, or twenty-seven cents a week. His fare included potatoes and unleavened bread made of a mixture of rye and Indian meal, but was mainly rice. He found that by working about six weeks in a year he could meet all his living expenses and have the entire winter and most of the summer free for study.

Thoreau considered his residence more favorable to thought and serious reading than a university. His neighbors were the birds, the trees, and the lake. The latter was entirely surrounded by woods; its opposite shore one-half mile away was his most distant horizon. He arose early, bathed in the lake, and sometimes sat in the "sunny doorway from sunrise till noon, rapt in a reverie, amidst the pines and hickories and sumachs, in undisturbed solitude and stillness."

In his front yard grew the strawberry, blackberry, blueberry, shrub-oaks, sand-cherry, and ground-nut. Hawks and wild pigeons circled about. The fishhawk brought up fish from the pond's glassy surface, and flitting reed-birds bent the sedge. On summer evenings the whippoorwills sat on a stump by the cottage door or upon the ridge-pole of the house and "chanted their vespers half an hour." Later screech owls took up the doleful strain, and at the same time "all the shore rang with the trump of bullfrogs." There were also squirrels, screaming bluejays, wild geese, a laughing loon on the pond, and a fox barking in the night.

The nearest neighbor was a mile distant, but every day or two Thoreau strolled to the village to observe the habits of the villagers and at night after dark returned to the woods. Sometimes at midnight he fished from a boat by moonlight, or in the early morning hoed beans barefooted. The storm was music to his ear, and the gentle patter of raindrops was a "beneficient society." He found solitude wholesome and companionable. Thus he experimented with life, living simply and economically, searching for Nature's message to humanity. He went to the woods because he wished to live deliberately and deeply, to front only the essential facts of life, and see if he could learn what it had to teach.

As far as our present life is concerned there are lessons of value to be gained from the life and writings of this man. One is that of simple living. He thought that life is enriched by simplicity. In order to afford luxuries, man labors to the extent of making himself a machine, whereas if he would not want so many useless things he could work less and thus have more time to live. Food, clothing, shelter, and books were all the things Thoreau wanted. He cared nothing for wealth, a fine house, expensive clothing, tobacco, wines, or a single cent's worth of anything beyond the bare necessities. He was a complete nonconformist. He declined invitations to dinner parties. "They make their pride in making their dinner cost much; I make my pride in making my dinner cost little." He never voted, and refused to pay tax for the support of war. He considered newspaper reading a desecration and believed that conversation often degenerates into gossip. To obey conscience he thought more important than to obey law.

Notwithstanding Thoreau's emphasis on neglected principles, he went farther than necessary or advisable in his separation from social institutions. He never established a home, for he never married. He accepted few positions of responsibility where his powers of action could be put to use. He mingled too little in human society in this world and was not sufficiently interested in the world to come. Because he did not attend church, some of his remarks about the Bible and Christians show a misplaced emphasis. Terms sacred to the language of the Christian meant less to Thoreau than the flowers that grow in the woods. Recognizing to some extent the wretchedness of this world, he tried to live a pure and noble life by withdrawal from evil rather than through the transforming, sanctifying power of Christ.

As the end was approaching, due to the consuming fevers of tuberculosis, he said, "For joy I could embrace the earth. I shall delight to be buried in it." He had in a short life exhausted the capabilities of this world. He had enjoyed the natural life of man on earth, and he faced the end with no apparent vision of or concern for the future life.

IX

LOVE NOT THE WORLD

CHRISTINA ROSSETTI

IN a world of vanity and shadows, of melting snow-flakes, vanishing rainbows, and fleeting pleasures, lived a romantic maiden whose eye caught the gleams of a brighter, more enduring world. The present was real, but she was certain of an unknown land in a future kingdom that was more real. She possessed the superior vision, the heavenly perspective, and her sensitive soul throbbed with the glorified prospect before her. The brighter realm was so refulgent with divine glory that she could not love this present world of sin, suffering, and perishable things. Narrow was the only way to the celestial city in the far-away beautiful land; the broad road never ended there; so the saintly young lady, the author of the elysian thoughts, chose the narrow way. To lead her there she trusted herself to a Guide to whom she prayed, "Take my will, and take my heart, and take me, too."

Christina Georgina Rossetti lived most of her life in the heart of London. Her grandparents were Italian except one grandmother. The Rossetti family, consisting of the parents and four children, lived on a quiet street in a dingy neighborhood; their rooms were dark, and the furniture was modest; they had few English but many Italian visitors. The mother was a devout Christian, but the father, a teacher of Italian in London, was not. Although she took all her children to church, her sons soon discontinued; however, the daughters remained loyal church-goers all their lives. The children spent summer vacations with their grandparents thirty miles from London, which gave them an opportunity for coach rides and the enjoyment of flowers and animals.

The Rossettis were a brilliant family. Mrs. Rossetti and Maria Francesca were skilled governesses; Mr. Rossetti was a teacher and writer; Dante Gabriel was a painter and leading Victorian poet; William Michael was a critic of art and literature; and Christina is recognized as one of the greater religious poets of the English language.

Christina was deprived of some of the happiness and physical strength of youth because of serious illnesses. She became a sensitive, serious, dependent young woman, of slight figure, high forehead, delicate features, dreamy, hazel, mystic eyes, and a firm and sweet expression of face. Holman Hunt, an artist, persuaded her to sit for the figure of Christ in one of his paintings, and she sat for Mary, the mother of Jesus, in a painting by her brother, Dante Gabriel Rossetti, the painter and poet.

From the age of eleven her poetic gift was effectively employed, and when seventeen her grandfather, who operated a small printing press, printed a slender volume of her poems. These early verses revealed the sadness of her youth, her earnest self-denial of earthly pleasures and contempt for vain things of the world, and her longing for God and things eternal.

This unhappy world, fair and satisfying in appearance, was in reality "loathsome and foul with hideous leprosy," "a very monster void of love," and a beast "with pushing horns and clawed and clutching hands." Could the pure heart of Christina Rossetti love such a horrible beast?

No, indeed not! Though the world softly wooed her, she could not sell her soul or give away her life and youth. This picture of the world and this decision to remain unspotted were expressed in a poem, "The World," written at the age of twenty-four.

Because this virtuous maiden did not love a wicked world, her life and outlook were different. Her standard of self-denial and hope for reward are expressed as follows: "For the books we now forbear to read, we shall one day be endued with wisdom and knowledge; for the music we will not listen to, we shall join in the song of the redeemed. For the pictures from which we turn, we shall gaze unabashed on the Beatific Vision. For the companionship we shun, we shall be welcomed into angelic society and the communion of triumphant saints. For the amusements we avoid, we shall keep the supreme jubilee. For the pleasures we miss, we shall abide forever in the rapture of heaven."

Why should she read improper books and fiction tainted with evil? The Bible was her Book, her constant study and meditation. Her poetry glows with the language and ideas of the Scriptures. Six of her nine prose works and hundreds of her poems are devotional. She accepted literally and seriously the commandments and promises of the Bible. Even the novels of Thackeray were considered too worldly, but such books as the *Confessions of St. Augustine,* the *Imitation of Christ,* and *Pilgrim's Progress* she enjoyed. In later years she read more widely in the field of secular literature.

What are the benefits to be gained from worldly pleasures unless they are of definite moral value? She saw no benefits and could not permit herself to attend the theater. In a tour to France made by Christina, her

mother, and her brother William, she accompanied her
brother throughout the travels except when he went to
the theater; then she refused. Chess playing was abandoned because she felt herself too fond of winning. In
all matters of worldly indulgence her conscience was
very tender.

A group of artists who did not like the classicism
represented by Raphael inaugurated a movement called
the Pre-Raphaelite Brotherhood. One of the lesser members was James Collinson, an artist and a friend of Dante
Gabriel Rossetti, the guiding figure of the Pre-Raphael-
ites. Collinson became Christina's accepted lover. Although originally an Anglican, he affiliated himself
definitely with the Catholic Church, after which Christina considered it her duty to revoke the troth. She did
it with sorrow and reluctance and entered the shadows
that hovered long over her life. Her second lover was
Charles Gayley, a scholar and linguist, but he belonged
to no church and his views were not orthodox. Because
of his lack of religious conviction, she could not marry
him, although their mutual love continued throughout
life. Self-denial and suffering were preferable to anything that would detract from the love of God.

Neither the father, brothers, nor lovers of Christina
measured up to her Christian ideals and standards; it was
therefore consoling to meet a friend who had irreproach-
able religious views. To one such she wrote: "It is a
balm to my mother and me to hear a man of genius who
is also a Christian, who speaks of the personages and
facts of the Bible as of personages and facts, and who
brings love and devotion to his work for the glory of
God. Pray do not think me overbold in expressing my-

self, but you well know how many men of genius think and speak otherwise."

That Christina did not love the world was evident in various other ways. She had conscientious objections to nude figures in productions of art. The worldly society of her time she did not enter. She abhorred attendance at seances for the purpose of communication with the dead. While visiting Italy one winter she was thrilled with the sunny land of her fathers but could not think of residing there permanently, for she was unwilling to separate herself from the Anglican Church, and there was none in any Italian city. An advocate of women's rights wrote to Christina on the subject of woman suffrage. The correspondent was directed to the Bible for the poet's views on the duties and privileges of her sex.

Although Christina was never engaged as a resident governess, the occupation of her mother and sister, she did assist her mother in conducting a day school. Often in the midst of writing she went to visit the poor and sick, and frequently hours were devoted to making scrapbooks for children in hospitals. As long as her mother lived she took care of her, as she also did for each of her two aunts. Thus her life was spent in ministering to others, although she herself was an invalid at various times.

Literature was the supreme work and contribution of Christina Rossetti. Through her art she exalted the Christian faith, for she sought not only personal satisfaction in expression but the spiritual improvement of the reader and ever considered publication a great spiritual responsibility. To write for the Society for the Promotion of Christian Knowledge was to her a duty. Earnestly and thoroughly she performed the work requested by the society despite the meager compensation and endless physical pains involved. According to her creed, "the body must be sacrificed to the soul."

The spiritual and picturesque words she penned reveal the beauty of the divine life. A world of luscious fruits, fair flowers, and sweet breezes is also a world of death and doubt, of famine and failure, a world "befouled by evil" where some music is doleful and many amusements are foolish, where wealth wastes away, pleasures have wings, and love dies. But there is now and forever shall be a world of righteousness above where wealth is firm, pleasures are lasting, love is undying, and gladness unending.

> *I see the far-off city grand,*
> *Beyond the hills a watered land,*
> *Beyond the gulf a gleaming strand*
> *Of mansions where the righteous sup.*

"The downhill path is easy," but the road to heaven is uphill all the way. Christina chose the uphill way. If Christ suffered, she was willing to suffer. "Give me the lowest place," was her prayer. She could say with confidence,

> *He leads me by the thorny road*
> *Which is the road to heaven.*

As a pilgrim and stranger, Christina Georgina Rossetti lived humbly, looking ever for the city whose builder and maker is God. Through her sweet and graceful hymns, lyrics, and sonnets she has encouraged many to strive for the same goal.

X

CALM WOODS AND STILL WATERS

WILLIAM CULLEN BRYANT

A YOUNG man stood at the portals of a wide world, ready to chisel his career from the hard rocks of existence. In the eastern part of his native State was a city, a center of commerce and literature, where he wanted to live his life; but the size of the city and the means of the young man were at odds. He had no funds for self-support, and no one would know him in Boston. It was therefore more fitting that he seek some small village in his home region. Familiar and near was the hamlet, Plainfield, which he considered a suitable place for the exercise of his profession; so one December day he set out to make preliminary inquiries. Before the walk of seven miles was completed the evening shades had gatherd about him. Alone he walked toward approaching darkness, wondering what would become of him in the big, enigmatic world. He had no idea. While the dull moments passed he crossed the shadowy hills, feeling forlorn and desolate. Then suddenly he lifted his eyes and looked at the western sky, which was now flooded with the rosy afterglow of sunset. What majesty and splendor that flaming sea of western sky contained! Ah, some dark speck is floating there! It flutters like a bird — and truly it is a solitary waterfowl winging its flight along the illuminated horizon! Into the hazy distance the young man watched the lonely wanderer go. At last the form had disappeared, but the beauty of the scene lingered in his mind and awakened comforting reflections.

The flight of that little creature, alone and under risk of the fowler's gun, through the upper atmosphere of a cold winter day, was directed by an unerring, divinely given instinct. The religiously trained mind of William Cullen Bryant was impressed with the lesson of guidance and faith. After arriving at his lodging for the night he wrote the finest of his lyrics, "To a Waterfowl," concluding with the lesson this gracious experience had taught him:

> *He who from zone to zone,*
> *Guides through the boundless sky thy certain flight,*
> *In the long way that I must tread alone,*
> *Will lead my steps aright.*

Why was this youth of twenty-one so profoundly affected by an experience many a rustic passes by unheeded? A mere casual survey of his early environment and training gives the easy answer; in fact, he himself reveals the open secret. "While I stood in Nature's loneliness, I was with one with whom I early grew familiar, one who never had a frown for me, whose voice never rebuked me — ." From childhood, Nature was his friend; he listened to her voice, observed her calm and smiling face, and cultivated her friendship and her tutorship. He early became familiar with the benign influences of rural scenery. Cummington, his native hamlet, was surrounded with graceful trees and grassy meadows, gorgeous flowers and murmuring brooks, with a clear sky above. The farmhouse where he was born was considerably removed from other habitations and stood in the midst of hilly fields that sloped steeply down to a stony-bedded little stream. Magnificent was the scenery during the short summer season, but through a long, cold winter all was bleak and desolate except for artistic designs wrought by ice and snow.

In those early days western Massachusetts was a very sparsely settled region. Bryant attended the little district schools, participated in some few community entertainments, and, although of delicate physique, assisted with the tasks of the farm. But he found the companionship of books and Nature more pleasing. As soon as he was able to speak, his mother and grandmother taught him the Lord's Prayer and other little petitions. He often fervently supplicated, he says, that he might receive the gift of poetic genius and write enduring verses. Thus inclined, he early devoted himself to the poetic art and at the same time stored his mind with landscape pictures. In all seasons and hours he rambled through the deep woods, over hills and into ravines, exploring the secrets of field and forest until he was familiar with every brook and thicket and knew the name of every tree and flower.

As a sedate member of the bar, the poet still preferred to stroll about through the wild regions he loved. He never liked the drudgery of legal practice, and, disgusted at the failure of legal machinery to secure justice, decided to locate in New York City where prospects for literary work appeared hopeful. But before taking final leave he must commune once more with Nature. He entered the grand old woods that had been the sanctuaries of his musings, walked through the majestic solitudes, and beneath the verdant roof of trees worshiped the Creator.

Even after becoming editor of a city magazine, he missed his forest rambles and his heart was ever going back to the quiet rock-ribbed mountains. Accordingly he soon returned to his native hills for a brief visit, thereby escaping for a while "the city's stifling heat, its horrid sounds, and its polluted air." He heard again the glad voices of the birds and streams and felt afresh the celestial mountain wind.

The genial breezes of the country always awakened his harp to its finest tones; they inspired his most enduring praises of nature.

Throughout the years of a long life, William Cullen Bryant, poet of nature and editor of the most important newspaper of America, devoted many summer vacations to pedestrian tours. From study and care, from the city's jostling crowd, and from the busy toils of life he loved to steal away to the woodland where the lovely and lonely stream wandered along between beautiful green banks. There flowers were fairest and the summer air freshest. There he loved to muse and gaze on the river and listen to its wild, fairy music. In communion with his river-friend he expressed a desire to be free

> *To wander these quiet haunts with thee,*
> *Till the eating cares of earth should depart,*
> *And the peace of the scene pass into my heart.*

It was in the calm and aged woods that the poet found the highest satisfaction, the most appealing message of peace and rest, of love and beauty, and of eternity and infinity. There he was endued with a contentment, a tranquillity, and a gladness that made him forget all the misery and sorrow of the world. When wearied by the knotty, ever-distressing political and economic problems that confronted him as an editorial writer, the restful shady groves calmed his disturbed mind and soothed his chafed spirit. There the squirrels chirped merrily, the birds made music in the branches, insects danced in the warm beams, the rivulet rejoiced with continuous laughter, and from the blue sky the sun looked down and blessed the entire scene. There in the forest solitudes he felt the presence of God; the mighty trees spoke of His perpetual work of creation; their grandeur, strength, and grace were a witness to His perfection. In the shadow of the majestic trees the poet of the forest was inspired to compose his grandest hymns.

The flowers did not blossom in vain in our poet's world. In the early spring, sometimes before the snow was all gone, he loved to walk out into the woods and meet the modest and gentle yellow violet. And in the chilly autumn when woods were bare, the fringed gentian, looking heavenward with its "sweet and quiet eye," had charms and a message for him. Through all the intervening summer he was delighted with those fair and tender little children of the earth — the briar rose and the orchis, the goldenrod and aster, the windflower and sunflower.

There was an ever-recurring idea in the mind of Bryant that was supremely expressed at a very early age. One autumn day, already before he had left his parent's home at Cummington, he took a significant walk through his favorite timber lands. In reflective mood he observed the decaying trunks of trees and withered plant life. The flowers were in their graves, the glory of the earth had faded away. Death ruled all. The somber scene was suggestive of the whole earth as one vast sepulcher for the human race in all the length and breadth of its existence. Above this great tomb of man are the solemn decorations — hills, valleys, woods, rivers, stars, and sky. With stern impressiveness this idea remained long in his imagination. He saw the antiquity and duration of the earth, the unchangeableness and eternal youth of the river, in contrast to the brevity of human existence and the transitoriness of human affairs. The forests, the flowers, all nature, and life itself suggested death. So he praised death. He praised it for its function in purging the earth of evildoers, destroying the power of tyrants, warning pleasure-lovers, and serving as the great reformer of the world. He was saddened because death took away his sister, his father, and his friends; but he rejoiced that it was the dawn of a happier life. Youth looked at death, felt its solemnity, and did not fear.

Thus appears the most refreshing side of the life of the first American master of poetry. In age as in youth he was a walker, a traveler, and an observer. Six times he voyaged to Europe, journeyed frequently to the Illinois prairies where his brothers lived, took a trip to the South, to Cuba, to Mexico, interested always in the handiwork of the Creator and in the affairs of his fellowmen. A successful journalistic career yielded an ample income but little affected the poet's simple life. He purchased several farms, cultivated a garden, and meditated in the calm woods and by the still waters. He resolved to refresh his spirit "with the calm and beautiful of God's harmonious universe" and reflect upon "the mystery that links us to the greater world" of the future.

XI

TRIFLES MAKE PERFECTION

THOMAS GRAY

> *"Trifles make perfection and perfection is no
> trifle."*—Michael Angelo.

"WHERE ignorance is bliss, 'tis folly to be wise";
"to snatch a fearful joy"; "regardless of their
doom, the little victims play"; "the short and simple
annals of the poor"; "far from the madding crowd's
ignoble strife"; "the paths of glory lead but to the
grave"; "some mute inglorious Milton here may rest";
"along the cool sequestered vale of life"; "the unhonored
dead"; "to Fortune and to Fame unknown"; "large was
his bounty, and his soul sincere."

Have you ever heard these expressions? They are
taken from two short poems, an ode and an elegy, and
have become a part of the common speech of millions.
They have the honor of universal usage and will live,
because of their perfection, as long as men use the
English language.

The most perfect poem in the English language, say
the critics, is the "Elegy Written in a Country Church-
yard." The author, Thomas Gray, was a man who sought
perfection, who was never satisfied with his work, and
who allowed the publication of only twelve poems during his lifetime. In his preparation for a literary history
a friend, Horace Walpole, said that if he (Gray) pro-
ceeds in his usual pace he will read two years in order to

write the first page. Gray's literary perfection rested on a foundation of thorough Greek and Latin scholarship and a knowledge of English, French, and Italian masters.

"Gray never was a boy," said Walpole. Having been neglected by his wealthy, cruel, violent-tempered father, he was brought up by his mother and his aunt, who conducted a millinery shop. The mother sent her son to Eton where by means of her careful savings he was educated under the supervision of an uncle, an assistant master at Eton and a fellow at Cambridge. Always Gray held his mother in esteem and loving remembrance for her sacrifices on his behalf and requested in his will that he be buried beside her. At Eton his closest friends were Richard West, Horace Walpole, and Thomas Ashton. West was a nervous and precocious lad, as studious, brilliant, and delicate as Gray, and as proficient in literature. Gray was particularly shy but morally upright; though generally disregarding athletics, he wandered about the Eton fields and under the elms with Walpole or West. After leaving Eton, Gray and Walpole went to Cambridge while West entered Oxford. However, a correspondence continued.

At the university Gray quietly but diligently read Latin and Greek literature, although there were at that time no Greek textbooks for use in schools. He also wrote verses in these languages; those in Latin have been highly praised by scholars. It was merited praise, too, for in youth he had developed the habit of accuracy in details and attention to trifles. This habit, which he never lost, was not only evident in language work, but in the scientific and most minute observations of vegetable and animal life, which he early began under the guidance of his uncle.

Without taking a degree, Gray left Cambridge. Six months later his friend, Horace Walpole, son of the prime minister of England, offered to pay all expenses if Gray would join him in a grand tour on the continent. The three years' journey was the only foreign tour the poet ever took and was a valuable introduction to new and entertaining subjects of study. Cathedrals, palaces, ruins, cities, and rivers were carefully examined; ancient districts were thoroughly explored. The results of his observations were recorded in accurate and laborious notes and in fascinating letters. His most actively acquisitive mind was not satisfied with diligent research alone but demanded precision in listing the facts discovered. He investigated music, painting, architecture, statuary, antique sculpture, studied the languages of France and Italy, and observed the manners and customs of the people.

Shortly after returning to England, his friend, Richard West, lonely, disappointed, and ill, died at the early age of twenty-five. This was a profound grief and an unforgettable loss to which Gray gave expression in an attractive Latin poem and a graceful English sonnet. While spending the summer after the death of his friend in the village of Stoke Pogis with his uncle, the latter also died, whereupon Gray began writing the "Elegy."

Stoke Pogis, made famous by this great poem, lay scattered over a wide area and contained meadows, woodlands, paths, a few houses, and a church. The latter was a picturesque structure four miles from Eton and the Thames. For many years Gray's home was at West End House, a simple, two-story farmhouse near Burnham Beeches, Stoke Common, and Brockhurst Woods, where he loved to walk.

The "Elegy" had been begun under the stimulus of personal bereavement but was abandoned before completion. The poet, already a middle-aged man at twenty-five, was unfitted by temperament and feeble health for a profession. Compelled for a time to seek his own living, he went back to Cambridge where living was cheap and where the libraries of the university made study convenient. From now on he lived either at Cambridge or at Stoke Pogis with occasional periods of residence in London. His retirement at Cambridge was such that even students seldom saw him; particularly after achieving fame, people could catch a glimpse of him only after patient watching, and chiefly at the Rainbow Coffeehouse where he went to order books from the circulating library. Henceforth his was a life of perpetual study. During the next six years he applied himself intently to the consecutive study of the best Greek authors, which few scholars read in those days. His exact and extensive reading is evident in copious notes where he painstakingly arranged the contents and noted the peculiarities and difficult passages. Trifles make perfection even in the study of Greek.

Suddenly occurred the death of Gray's aunt, whom he much loved and who had been a great consolation to his mother. He remembered the unfinished "Elegy," returned to its composition, and completed it at Stoke Pogis in June, 1750. This matchless work has been called the flower of the literature of melancholy. It is an evening poem and a graveyard poem, expressing true hope in God. It expresses sympathy for and shows the worth of the lives of humble, simple peasants. Immediately popular, it was soon translated into ancient and modern languages, became the most widely admired

English poem, and is said to have influenced the poetry of all Europe. It makes a universal appeal because it sets forth thoughts common to all mankind in the presence of death and tombstones, and because of its charming melody, metrical skill, and dignified and perfect expression. No one can improve it, and no one thinks it needs improvement. If it is "the most perfect poem in the English language," it is so because the poet had an eye for trifles as well as for unity, proportion, and finish in the entire structure. His striving for perfection is evident in the careful choice of words. Out of the words he built the line, out of the lines he built the stanza, and out of stanzas he constructed the completed poem. He worked by the method of detail and linked pictures together in the classical manner. Even his handwriting is significant. Says a student of Gray, "I have seen and transcribed many a page of it, but I do not recollect to have noticed a single carelessly written word or even letter. The mere sight of it suggests refinement, order, and infinite pains."

One of the few poets entitled to the character of the sublime, the most finished artist of all English poets, one who has "attained the highest degree of splendor of which poetical style seemed to be capable"—these things were said because the same high standards prevailed in all Gray's poetry. On "The Bard" he worked long and slowly "as though he were a sculptor, deliberately pointing and chiselling a statue." As a result, this poem was long unrivaled for "sublimity and pomp of vision."

Thomas Gray has been designated "perhaps the most learned man in Europe" and the greatest scholar among English poets except Milton. He possessed boundless intellectual curiosity and a comprehensive mind. With

customary precision and thoroughness he studied old
Saxon poetry, translated romantic lyrics from Gaelic and
Scandinavian sources, and wrote learned essays on meter.
He had read the leading historians of England, France,
and Italy in their own languages, possessed extensive
knowledge of botany and zoology, and had made the
most perfect account of English insects. His notes and
papers show thorough knowledge of painting, architecture, gardening, geography, and heraldry. Excellent
taste in music had been developed by a study of Italian
masters; antiquities delighted him; he knew the literature of the art of cooking. He kept notes concerning the
weather and recorded the dates when the earliest spring
flowers and birds appeared. Details, jots, and tittles,
trifles! Yes, but by them the scholar wins or loses.

One can be an artist in letter writing. Gray's letters
reveal his humor, melancholy, seriousness, classical taste,
and elegant style; they have charm, simplicity, and "perfection of ease and grace"; they contain striking descrip-
tions and valuable criticisms of literature.

Regretting his unproductiveness in literature due to
lack of health, Gray on one occasion spoke complainingly,
but checked himself, considering it wrong "to repine at
the decrees of Providence." Religious subjects in his
writings were approached with piety, and atheistic
writers were strongly opposed. A young friend, coming
to bid farewell before leaving for a continental tour, was
advised not to pay tribute to Voltaire by visiting him.
Although lacking in missionary zeal, Gray was considered a believer in Christianity and a good man. One
might wish he had had more Christian enthusiasm, but,
being ever a moralist, he perhaps knew the value of the
highest perfection, perfection in character, which is
obtained alone through faith in Christ.

XII

CONQUERING THROUGH PATIENCE

LOUISA MAY ALCOTT

A PROVERB says that patience conquers the world. The beautiful life of the popular story writer, Louisa May Alcott, teaches much about the value of patience, for she conquered not only the world but likewise herself.

Louisa May Alcott was a member of a very interesting family. Her father was Amos Bronson Alcott, teacher and philosopher, who was an unusually fascinating talker, a very skilful teacher, and a superior writer. Although he had modern and advanced views of education, the schools he started did not prosper, for many people did not believe in his progressive methods and took their children from him. As a result, the Alcott family was poor and was continually moving. The father, though possessing superior abilities, was at times compelled to be a day laborer.

Louisa had three sisters — Anna, Elizabeth, and May. Practically the only teacher Louisa ever had was her father. He was much interested in his little girls, took care of them, taught them daily, and had a concern for every detail of their childhood lives.

One of Louisa's early achievements was gaining control over her own disposition. She had a tempestuous nature, a violent temper, and but little patience. In her quarrels with her sisters she was generally not the one to yield. When she was about four, her father referred to her as a guideless creature, proudly, adventurously following the objects of her desires on the impetuous stream of instinct.

"Hers is the wild exuberance of a powerful nature." He noted her ungovernable energy and passionate obstinacy and felt that he needed to use "decided measures to check the stormy current of her being."

Louisa's mother understood the forceful, tempestuous nature of her daughter, and helped her in conquering her temper. As soon as the father had taught the girls to write, they were required to keep a journal of their daily thoughts and deeds. Mother often put loving notes, full of encouragement and advice into Louisa's journal or elsewhere. When about thirteen, Louisa had a great desire for a little room of her own but had to wait a long time until such an arrangement could be made. She addressed a little note to her mother, telling how she tried to be contented, although she so much wanted and often thought about the little room. Mother wrote a little letter in return to express her thankfulness for Louisa's tender love and willing obedience to Mother and her patience and kindness to her sisters. "Go on trying, my child; God will give you strength and courage, and help you fill each day with words and deeds of love."

Such sympathetic helpfulness on the mother's part did much in assisting Louisa to control the disturbing elements of her early life and in brightening the periods of gloom and sadness. And there were also other things that helped. One was the happy hours of play. When she was an active little girl of eleven years, the Alcotts moved to Fruitlands, for Mr. Alcott had been compelled to give up his school in Boston. Here at Fruitlands, a little hillside farm with a dilapidated farmhouse, she could run over the hills, roll hoops, watch the flapping black crows, see plants grow from tiny seeds, and gather blackberries from the corners of the farm. Later the family lived in Concord where they had a pleasant house, a big barn, and a garden full of trees. In one wing of the large wooden house Louisa had at last the little room she so long desired. In this house the children acted out the stories their father told them in the evening and in the barn they played games and also dramatized stories. The Alcott girls were often assisted in their games by the Emerson children — Ellen, Edith, and Edward — and by the Hawthorne children — Una, Julian, and Rose; for Emerson and Hawthorne were both Concord residents.

Then, too, work made a contribution in acquiring patience. Childhood was not all a carefree period, for there was plenty of work to do. Fruitlands was something of a transcendental farming experiment carried on by Mr. Alcott and several assistants. Hence there were more to provide for than just the Alcotts. The girls had to assist Mother with the cooking, washing, and ironing, and they also helped rake the hay, husk corn, and do chores. This was the beginning of Louisa's career as a hard worker.

Although the Alcott home was rich in generosity and love, it was poor in worldly goods. While living at Fruitlands, the family endured much suffering and was restricted to a vegetable diet. In those days the Alcott children had for breakfast, unleavened bread, porridge, and water; for dinner, bread, vegetables, and water; and for supper, bread, fruit, and water.

Such poverty at times really added to Louisa's lack of patience. Once while passing through a period of depression, she wrote: "My quick tongue is always getting me into trouble, and my moodiness makes it hard to be cheerful, when I think how poor we are, how much worry it is to live, and how many things I long to do — I never can. So every day is a battle, and I'm so tired I don't want to live, only its cowardly to die till you have done something."

This constant battle against poverty, while revealing the impatience of her spirit, was also a means of giving purpose to her energies. There was place here to apply her forcefulness and perseverance. She observed the strenuous toil of her mother and saw how harshly people treated her father and did not appreciate his talents as a teacher. In her little room of the large house at Concord, Louisa had already begun to think about the future, and planned to do something some day for the parents and sisters whom she loved. Now a young woman, she proposed to earn money and give her parents and sisters comforts they had long been denied. Employment, however, was difficult to obtain, but she persisted in carrying out her noble resolution even though things often went against her. One of the few remunerative lines of work she was able to find was teaching. Her first school, which she taught at the age of sixteen, was held in a barn, and the Emerson children constituted the greater number of her pupils. She soon understood the minds of children and won their hearts by telling them fascinating stories. She had a great determination to succeed, but was too restless, impatient, and impetuous to like the work. It was, however, one of the main sources of income for a number of years.

At an early age, Louisa had begun to write stories for her sisters and neighboring children. These first stories were flower fables. One of them, written for Ellen Emerson when Louisa was sixteen, was found by her father, who showed it to a publishing friend. It was accepted and published, and the author received five dollars. In those early days she also wrote tales of adventure, and while at work kept thinking of ideas and plots for other stories. On another occasion her father took one of her stories to a friend who was an editor. He said, "Tell Louisa to

stick to her teaching. She is never going to be a writer."
"I will not stick to my teaching. I will be a writer," she
firmly declared, and she later contributed to this same
editor's magazine. The publication of the flower fable written at the age of sixteen was the beginning of her career
as an author, but she still depended on teaching and sewing
as the main sources of her income.

The patient endurance of Miss Alcott was shown in
many ways during her early years of womanhood. At
various times she went to Boston seeking work and facing
the world alone with but a limited amount of money. She
accepted almost any tasks she could find and wrote stories
during leisure hours. A woman of her ambitions met many
disappointments, and sometimes she was sad, lonely, and
homesick. Even though very busy, there was time to teach
in a little mission Sunday School. Sunday evenings were
often spent at the home of Theodore Parker, whose church
she attended. Observing the determined spirit of his young
friend, he said, "Louisa is going to succeed."

During the Civil War, being much interested in the
abolition of slavery, she volunteered as a hospital nurse and
was accordingly sent to a hospital in Georgetown. Once a
large hotel, this building with dirty floors and windows
was soon crowded with wet and muddy wounded soldiers
who were placed on rickety iron cots with dark mattresses
and hard pillows. Miss Alcott washed and dressed the
wounds, spoke words of cheer to sick and dying patients,
made beds, carried trays, and rushed about the building
for bandages and adhesive tape. She was compelled to
take care of measles, typhoid, diptheria, and pneumonia.
The uncleanness, the lack of fresh air, and the strain of
the work were injurious to health, and the self-sacrificing
nurse gradually became a victim of typhoid. After less

than six months of strenuous service she was obliged to leave, and she never completely regained her former robust health.

The extent to which Louisa May Alcott controlled her own spirit and applied her powers for the happiness of others becomes more evident when one recognizes her achievements. Finding that she could do more than write short stories, she wrote books of wholesome fiction, which at once attracted the attention of young people. Publishers became so insistent for her work that she was utterly unable to supply the demand. She used the money from her writing in making her father and mother comfortable and in educating relatives. She paid up the family debts, equipped her father's library, sent her artist sister abroad for further training, and contributed to other worthy causes. Her purpose was achieved — the dispersion of poverty from the family. The more than twenty-five books written by Louisa May Alcott give tribute to her conquering patience.

And through patience she achieved a larger end — the winning of hosts of friends. She was a true friend to the members of her family, contributed much to the happiness of each, and gave them lasting places of remembrance in her writings, which are largely based on family experiences. One of her best friends was Emerson, whose library she freely used; and another was Thoreau, from whom she learned much about nature. Hers was an ever widening circle of friends, both in place and time. The children of America have now for three generations loved her books. The children of the leading European countries have through translations learned to consider Miss Alcott their friend. She gave millions of young people years of strenuous but patient, loving service.

XIII

A GALLERY OF PORTRAITS

WILLIAM LAW

FROM the midst of the easy-going life of the eighteenth century, a remarkable man, conscientious and God-fearing, sent out a clarion call to bring back Christians to their high privilege of living devout and holy lives. William Law's *A Serious Call to a Devout and Holy Life,* recommending a life of strict devotion, powerfully influenced John Wesley, Charles Wesley, George Whitefield, and many others, and contributed much toward the rise and spread of the evangelical revival.

In this most effective book are more than twenty-five portraits illustrative of views expressed. The right use of time and money is illustrated in the character of Miranda, a young woman concerned with the problem of how to meet the requirements of God in the best and happiest use of time and fortune. Her one reason for doing or not doing anything is the will of God. Her fine breeding consists in the fact that she has renounced the world to follow Christ in the exercise of humility, charity, devotion, abstinence, and heavenly affections. Formerly she lived a worldly life, patronizing the theater, public dances, and the latest fashions; but since her conversion she entirely altered her behavior.

After the death of her parents Miranda is one of two sisters to receive two hundred pounds a year. Of this amount she spends less than ten pounds upon herself, for she regards her fortune the gift of God, and to be used accordingly. She begins each day with God by offering early prayers and interceding for those who are still asleep, thus seeming a guardian angel to all about her. In her diet she is abstemious, remembering that hers is not an earthly race but a heavenly one of purity and holiness. Most of her money is spent in charity for others. Among things done in a charitable way are: she has set up nearly twenty poor tradesmen who failed in business, and saved as many more from failing. She has educated several poor children. She provides the needs of workers and their families during times of illness, and also helps support poor families that cannot earn enough to make ends meet. She relieves the most abandoned sinners in times of adversity, thus sometimes inducing them to repentance. Poor people she continually relieves. If, for instance, someone loses a cow or horse, or is robbed, she immediately gives them the full value of their loss. She constantly helps old people who can no longer work by allowing them somewhat more than the wages they formerly received. Thus the infirm can serve God in peace and tranquillity of mind. Even toward beggars she has compassion and feels it proper to give alms to her enemies.

At night one must answer for all the actions of the day, thinks Miranda; for this reason she does not idle away her time but employs it in things necessary. With her own hands she makes clothing for the poor of the neighborhood.

Daily she studies the Holy Scriptures, especially the New Testament, and observes herself to see whether she measures up to its doctrines. While reading the New Testament, she imagines herself at the feet of the Savior and the Apostles. Outside of the Bible she most delights in reading the lives of pious persons and eminent saints. She also reads other books and buys especially those that describe the inward holiness of the Christian life.

In contrast to the portrait of Miranda, a model of Christian perfection, is that of her sister, Flavia, who also receives two hundred pounds a year but practices charity in an altogether different spirit. Flavia considers the poor people cheats and liars, whom alms would encourage in their evil ways. If anyone asks her to make a contribution she tosses a coin in case she likes the person or is in the right mood and explains that due to her milliner's bill she cannot give more. She follows the fashions and buys all the books of wit and humor.

Usually Flavia attends church and appears orthodox, but is only half as careful of her soul as of her body. If a mere pimple rises on her face or a gnat stings her, she keeps her room two or three days. Often she sits in bed doing fine work until noon and thus neglects her morning devotions. About half her time is spent in bed and most of the remaining half in eating, drinking, dressing, visiting, reading, and hearing plays and romances, and attending operas and balls. On Sunday afternoons she can tell her visitors all the petty happenings, such as who is rude and ill-natured, who is vain and foppish, who is in love, how cross Lucius is to his wife, and what games are most popular.

The irreligion, folly, and vanity of her whole life is due to the use she makes of her money. For this reason she greatly regards her body and is careless of things that might benefit her soul. Were it not for the imprudent use of her money, she might be humble, serious, devout, a lover of good books, an admirer of prayer and

retirement, diligent in good works, full of charity and
the love of God. Her life shows that not only gross sins,
but the imprudent use of lawful and innocent things,
can hinder progress in religion. Law comments that he
will not take upon himself to say that Flavia cannot be
saved but that there is no ground in the Scripture to that
effect, for her entire life is contrary to the practices the
gospel makes necessary to salvation.

Law maintains that the happiest life is the one that is
wholly devoted to God. The misery of those left to the
folly of their own passions is shown in the case of Flatus,
rich and healthy, but ever restless and in search of
happiness. Continually he is taking up a new project
and leaving an old one, but never finds satisfaction.
Starting out in life a young man, he took great delight
in fine clothes, and spared no expense with the best
tailors. This did not bring the expected happiness, so
he took up the playing of dice and other games. Next
he sought the diversions of the town, and for more than
a year talked of nothing but women, parties, and balls.
Then he turned to hard drinking, which he enjoyed for
some time; but finally, becoming ill, he abandoned the
happiness of being drunk. Later through several years
he found happiness in hunting; in this sport he became
so enthusiastic that he surpassed everybody else in the
quality of his dogs. Upon each change he ridiculed what
he was fond of before. During a year later his sole
delight was in horseback riding, for which he acquired a
great variety of horses, saddles, and bridles. But he
grew tired of riding, and the happiest thing he could then
think about was foreign travel. Afterwards, unable to
endure the impertinence of foreigners, he diligently
studied Italian grammar through one entire year. In all

these attempts after worldly enjoyments, and the follies, anxieties, and delusions connected therewith, Flatus found no happiness, for true happiness, Law points out, can only be found in a life devoted to God.

There is a learned man, ingenious and well versed in literature, named Octavius, who has reached the closing days of his life and feels that he had no more than a year to live. He says that since he is in physical decline he must leave the taverns and furnish his own cellar with the best wine and that he must now limit his many companions to three or four cheerful ones. Shortly after making these declarations Octavius dies. A young man, Eugenius, had heard the above remarks, and seeing how poorly and meanly the learned Octavius left the world, resolved to devote his life wholly unto God. Eugenius had envied the great learning, linguistic skill, and speaking ability of Octavius, but when he saw how foolishly the distinguished man, who had no religion, talked, he saw how comfortless is death without piety.

Another apparently good man, but lacking in Christian devotion, is Negotius. For thirty years he has been an important business man, writing fifty or sixty letters in a week to all parts of Europe. He contributes liberally to all enterprises but has never felt the necessity for piety; too many other important things occupy his mind. Although Negotius seems to know what he is doing, he has no one general, deliberately chosen aim in life, worthy of his labor and pains. Some comfort is derived from the fact that he has more business than other people, that he is growing richer and will die richer than any other person of his business ever did. Most people would have thought him a happy man, for he was sober, prudent, rich, prosperous, generous, and charitable. But had he lived a life of humility, piety, and self-denial, a life like that of Christ devoted to God, of prayer, and filled with the love of God, he would have gained much and lost little.

The most important portrait in this gallery is that of the good country parson, the unblamable minister of the gospel, Ouranius. This holy man watches, labors, and prays for the people of a small village; he loves them all as he loves himself, and prays for them all as he prays for himself. By often appearing before God as an intercessor, he has learned the great value of souls. He can never love or do enough for his flock. He visits everybody in his parish, encourages their virtues, assists them with advice, and discovers their manner of life and the state of their souls that he may more intelligently intercede for them. He has prayed away his former haughty temper, his contempt for foolish people, and has now the greatest tenderness for sinners. Now, instead of being impatient with rude or perverse members of his flock, he desires to be upon his knees in prayer to God for them. His tenderness in reproving, affection in exhorting, and vigor in preaching result from prayer to God before reproving, exhorting, and preaching.

At first Ouranius had considered his little village as disagreeable as a prison, but now through great devotion to God he takes much comfort in the solitude of his parish. He gladly attends upon the poorest people, and watches daily over the weak. Talking with poor and lowly ones about the kingdom of heaven, he now thinks the best conversation in the world. That his prayers may avail much with God, he practices all the arts of holy living.

By such and similar portraits William Law reveals the shortcomings of Christians, admonishing them to live lives of humility, self-denial, and piety; to avoid pride, covetousness, and ambition; to live wholly unto God by employing talents, time, and money according to His will; and to devote all of life to the honor and glory of God in all possible ways.

XIV

THE FIFTH COMMANDMENT

THOMAS CARLYLE

MOTHER had prepared his clothes and other neces-sities. She had made plans for his laundering and for supplies of food to be sent to him. It was her oldest son, Tom, that was leaving home. He was only fourteen, or rather one month less, and was now ready to turn his steps toward Edinburgh, the capital city one hundred miles away. She implored him to fear God and to read his Bible. The time was November, very early on a misty morning and still dark, when he left his native village, his simple home, his brothers and sisters, and his loving par-ents. Father and Mother went with him the first few miles until he joined a slightly older youth who knew the way. Walking was the most inexpensive way to travel, and the lads could make twenty or thirty miles a day.

Ecclefechan, a village of five hundred people in the western lowlands of Scotland, was the birthplace of Thomas Carlyle. He was the son of James and Margaret Carlyle, plain, hardworking, honest, and religious Scottish peasants. They had seen unusual talents in their son and decided to have him educated for the service of the church. It was therefore necessary to send him to the University of Edinburgh. Long had his mother hesitated to have her oldest boy leave home at the early age of fourteen to live in a strange distant city where he was utterly unknown and where she would not be able to supervise his lodgings and general care. But he had already obtained practically all the schooling his native region afforded, and if he were to progress in his training, Edinburgh was the logical destination.

This was no ordinary lad whom James and Margaret Carlyle hopefully planned to have educated; they themselves were above the ordinary. Only by severe struggle could the father gain a livelihood. He became an expert mason and built the thatched stone cottage where his son was born. The houses he built, wrote Thomas Carlyle, "stand firm and sound to the heart all over his little district." The mother could read her Bible but could not write. She taught herself penmanship in order to write to her son in college and direct him toward things religious. There were nine children in the family. They were brought up on oatmeal, milk, and potatoes, and by precept and example were taught to work. The father read the Bible in family worship, and on Sunday all attended the village church.

Having been taught arithmetic by his father and letters by his busy mother, Thomas at five entered the village school and impressed his parents with abilities above the average. James Carlyle's brother, an assistant who did the calculating in the masonry business, observed the arithmetical proficiency of the little Thomas and confessed that the lad was at least his equal if not his superior. "I don't grudge thee thy schooling now, Tom," said his father. At ten Thomas entered Annan Academy, six miles from Ecclefechan, where he showed his skill in mathematics. Shy and sensitive, he was persecuted because his mother had taught him not to strike back. When the decision was made to send him to the University at Edinburgh, the neighbors said to James Carlyle, "Educate a boy, and he grows up to despise his ignorant parents." We shall soon see whether the neighbors were right in this case.

At Edinburgh the young student lodged near the school and attended the large classes. He was sometimes shabbily dressed and insufficiently nourished and already showed his characteristic generosity and simplicity combined with sarcasm, irony, and an inclination to undervalue others. Soon he detected what some of the professors thought about accepting the Scriptures and during vacation asked his mother questions that kept her awake at night weeping and praying for her son. But he kept most of his doubts to himself and in his distress read books on the evidences of Christianity.

During these four university years the mother sent her son a monthly box filled with oatmeal, potatoes, and butter, which was about all he had to eat. When the summer vacations came he tramped back to his happy Ecclefechan home in Dumfriesshire. Thomas was the pride of her heart and the hope of her expectations, and she never failed to admonish him in the ways of the Christian religion. He well knew the sacrifices his parents were making for him.

Upon leaving the university, he determined to become self-supporting. His former school, Annan Academy, needed a mathematics teacher, and Thomas succeeded in securing the position. After teaching two years at Annan, he taught two years at Kirkaldy. While teaching he read Hume and Gibbon, noted enemies of orthodox Christianity; as a result his faith in miracles and in the foundations of Christianity was shattered and he decided not to become a minister. Teaching also proved a disagreeable work, and after four years of it he abandoned the profession.

He went to Edinburgh, rented a room, took private pupils in mathematics and astronomy, and began to study German. From teaching he had saved $850 — enough for several years' support, but his mother still sent him oatmeal, butter, socks, shirts, and other home products. The most struggling years of his strenuous life were now upon him. He was poor and unknown. The meager nourishment during a school career had seriously disturbed his digestive apparatus and before long his dyspepsia was like "a rat gnawing at the pit of his stomach." Religious doubt and mental gloom oppressed him. His father had not favored the abandonment of teaching but now and through all his subsequent distresses remained silent. He did not criticize nor even show disappointment, which Carlyle ever gratefully remembered. His mother was deeply disappointed because he had turned against service in the church but she continued to urge him toward religion. Nearly every letter from her urged him to God. "Oh, my dear, dear son, I would pray for a blessing on your learning. I beg with all the feelings of an affectionate mother you would study the Word of God, which He has graciously put in our hands." And in the postscript to one letter she adds: "Do make religion your great study, Tom; if you repent it, I will bear the blame forever."

Permanent employment was at this time Carlyle's great desire. He thought about civil engineering and began the study of law but found himself not sufficiently interested in either. Literature seemed the most suitable field. He found literary employment as contributor to an encyclopedia and in translating from French and German. His perplexity and black despondency grew no less; in fact his religious struggle grew more intense and torturing; he was bowed down with a "load of woes" and seemed to be "dying by inches." One June day on Leith's walk, Edinburgh, while thinking of man's eternal destiny, Carlyle suddenly acquired thoughts and an attitude that fixed his religious faith. This he called his "rebirth." He had feared death and eternal separation from his devout mother. He now banished fear, established himself in belief in God, and became a bitter foe of atheism, but he did not accept the revelation of God as taught by the church. He tried to assure his greatly concerned mother that his faith was similar to hers, only differently expressed; however, she based her life on the creed of the church, and he did not. Carlyle believed that God controlled the universe, and he tried to reform society in harmony with God's standard of human government, but he did not know God as a personal friend and thought some of the New Testament teachings absurd.

After Carlyle's marriage to Jane Welsh, he lived for a number of years at Craigenputtock, a house and farm miles from any other human dwelling, "a green oasis in a desert of heath and rock." Mrs. Carlyle wrote: "It is the stillest, solitariest place that it ever entered upon your imagination to conceive." "In the silence of the barren hills" Carlyle was free to meditate, read, and write all day, to wander regardless of cold or rain among the hills, or on fair days to ride horseback with Jane. His brother, Alick, took care of the thousand-acre farm. During the six years at Craigenputtock the memorable book *Sartor Resartus,* was written.

Carlyle's letters home never ceased as long as his parents lived. He told his mother all about his health, his writings, and his daily employment, and often, on completing an article for the magazines, went back to the home folks for several days. When he moved to London for the benefit of his literary career, parting from his mother was his greatest grief. He wrote that "she was the truest Christian believer I have ever met with; nay, I might almost say the only true one."

The same love and concern was shown for all the members of the family. He advised his two brothers, John and Alexander, what to read, and generally provided funds for John's medical education. At the death of his sister, Margaret, he deeply mourned, and said it was "the most poignant sorrow I had yet felt." At the death of his father he could not return to Scotland for the funeral, so he wrote to his mother and brothers and sisters the most comforting letter:

"My dear Brothers and Sisters, sorrow not, I entreat you; sorrow is profitless and sinful; but meditate deeply every one of you on this. None of us but started in life with far greater advantages than our dear Father had; we will not weep for him; but we will go and do as he has done. Could I write my books as he built his houses, and walk my way so manfully through this shadow-world, it were more than all my hopes. Neither are you, my beloved Mother, to let your heart be heavy. Faithfully you toiled by his side, bearing and forbearing as you both could; all that was sinful and of the earth has passed away; all that was true and holy remains forever, and the parted shall meet together again with God. Amen!"

One of the greatest calamities of Carlyle's life was the utter destruction of the first volume of his *French Revolution* after having expended five months of agonizing labor, or as he said, "of steadfast, occasionally excessive, and always sickly and painful toil." It was loaned to an interested friend, John Stuart Mill, who carelessly left it lying about; a servant mistook it for waste paper and destroyed it. Carlyle was compelled to

rewrite the entire volume, which was completed six
months later; it was, said the author, the ugliest task of
his life. Writing was ever to Carlyle an extremely difficult task; his books "were written in sore tribulation."
The famous *French Revolution* was written amidst alter-
nating hope and fear. "Oh, that I had faith! Oh, that I
had! Then were there nothing too hard or too heavy
for me. Cry silently to thy inmost heart to God for it.
Surely He will give it thee." This lack of faith was what
so distressed his mother. After three years living in a
"fire-blaze," the brilliant *French Revolution* was finished
and the writer went back to Scotland to his old home
and family. "You have not," he announced to the world,
"had for two hundred years any book that came more
truly from a man's very heart."

After the death of Carlyle's father, his great concern
for his mother had increased. A typical letter on the
occasion of her birthday began: "My ever-loved Mother,
I salute you with my affection once more," and he
thanked her for all her unwearied care over him. To his
brother, Alick, now in Canada, he wrote: "Let us be
thankful for many blessings such as fall to the lot of
few. Good Parents whom you can honor, it is the foundation of all good for a man." Shortly before the death of
his mother he wrote: "Whatever other things have gone
wrong with me, the love of my true Mother never went
wrong. . . . I think the older I grow, the more entirely
I feel myself my Father's and my Mother's son, and have
more and more reason to be thankful, and piously proud,
that I had such parents." At the time of this writing he
was already fifty-eight years of age.

When his mother died he was engaged in the gigantic
task of writing *Frederick,* a historic work requiring

thirteen years and many thousand miles of traveling. It was his sorest task, a "desperate dead-lift pull" that "taxed almost to extinction the failing vitality of age." During the process of composition, his mother now being dead, he wrote in his journal: "Oh, pious Mother! kind, good, brave, and truthful soul as I have ever found in this world, your poor Tom, long out of his school-days now, has fallen very lonely, very lame and broken in this pilgrimage of his; and you cannot help him or cheer him by a kind word anymore." Said one who knew him personally, "Much of the profound sadness in him came, I think, from his utter disbelief."

Thomas Carlyle was a man terribly in earnest, a fighter for great social reforms, and a powerful and fascinating writer. Especially since the World War are his social, economic, and political doctrines investigated. Although strongly influenced by the faith of his fathers, he did not fully follow it; however, if ever mortal kept the fifth commandment, it was Thomas Carlyle. After his death he was not buried with England's great in Westminster Abbey, London, as friends had wished; but, as he had requested, in the little Ecclefechan grave-yard near the graves of his pious peasant ancestors.

XV

THE USE OF IDEAS

RALPH WALDO EMERSON

ARCHIMEDES, the ancient Greek scientist and mathematician, in speaking of the lever, declared, "Give me a place to stand, and I will move the world." But Joseph Conrad, a modern English writer, with more practical truth, says, "Give me the right word and the right accent, and I will move the world." He states that such mere words as "glory" or "pity," when shouted with perseverance, with ardor, with conviction, by their sound alone have set whole nations in motion. In "The Poet," Tennyson tells how the words of one poor poet "shook the world." Because words were fitly spoken, "truth was multiplied on truth; the world like one great garden showed."

Twelve days before an American youth was nineteen years old, he reviewed the history of his intellect and lamented the meagerness of his accomplishments. While believing that perhaps he possessed as many ideas as other young people his age, he after all felt a goading sense of emptiness and wasted capacity, and that instead of adding to his gems of knowledge he was too content to admire present limited achievements. "Idolatrous of glory," he had in early youth nourished "brilliant visions of future grandeur"; now he saw his inferiors and juniors surpassing him in paths to learning, wisdom, and fame, and wondered whether he should resign every aspiration to belong to the family of giant minds that rule the world after their bodies are decayed. He emphatically answered, "No!" This young man, Ralph Waldo Emerson, was not satisfied in an effort to move the world with words only; he aspired to the domain of wisdom and ideas.

And he was destined to become a master of ideas, for, despite his self-reproach, he fitted himself by early creating a literary atmosphere, although environed by poverty as well as culture. At the Boston Latin School, where rhetoric was then the popular subject, he spent his leisure hours in writing and won the approval of teachers and friends for graceful compositions in prose and verse. With his entrance into Harvard came development in the range and quality of ideas in addition to the power of their expression. He read extensively in accordance with personal tastes but not always as professors commanded. At Harvard was begun the practice of privately recording thoughts gathered from reading and thinking; these writings, continuing until the age of seventy-five, constitute his journals, and are the source of ideas used later in lectures and essays. While still a student, ability to express ideas was rewarded by two prizes for dissertations and one for declamation.

Thought and physical activity were not closely related in the life of young Emerson, for bodily inertness prevented him from participation in athletics. Although reserved and often solitary, yet beneath his grave and slender form was an independent mind actively at work, and he was an interested member of various school societies.

Soon came the time for sharing ideas with fellow men. The common way was the schoolroom, which he tried but found irksome and oppressive. As instructor of young women in a private school, he was easily embarrassed, was timid about his French, and did not like mathematics. His thoughts were occupied with philosophical speculations concerning the meaning of life, man, and the universe, and leisure hours he devoted to reading and writing. Teaching, he considered a failure; in later years, however, upon an occasion of reunion with former students, they sincerely commended him for his work as their teacher.

What is an education for if not to equip one for the dissemination of ideas? Not being disposed to endure mediocrity, he turned without regret or hesitation from professorial dignity to that of the ministerial office, with a detour, however, through the Harvard Divinity School. There his career was interrupted by a weak and collapsing physical constitution, necessitating an excursion to the south for rest. After spending the winter in a milder climate, he returned and resumed his studies but was ordained to the ministry before the completion of his course. It was now his business to diffuse the ideas of the Christian religion.

It has been said that Emerson never acquired a thorough knowledge of theology and that his brief studies in the divinity school were not thorough. Most of his early reading in literature and history had been secular rather than Christian; besides he lived in a time of growing religious liberalism among the Puritan descendants of New England. Also his ardent desire for intellectual freedom and independence roused an attitude of rebellion toward the traditional beliefs and forms of the Christian church, which he felt restricted him. As a result he had neither a good foundation nor the proper attitude for a successful Christian ministry. After he

decided that the communion was not meant to be observed with the literal use of sacred emblems and
announced that he would no longer officiate at that
service, his resignation became necessary.

The man of ideas had failed again. Teaching he had
found uncongenial. He was still afflicted with weak eyes
and rheumatism and threatened with consumption. His
wife had died soon after marriage, and now he was
separated from the vocation of his youthful choice. Certain ideas had been pursued so long and so far that he
could no longer believe in a personal God, a historic
Christ, nor an authoritative church. Apparently he had
lost almost the last vestige of the Christian faith.

Escape from these dark clouds was sought by a voyage
to Europe, where he visited the Italian centers of art
and religion, gazed upon the treasures of galleries and
cathedrals, and revitalized his bookish ideas by direct
contact with the spirit of the old world. In Paris he
loitered to observe with care the inexhaustible riches of
nature as exhibited in the famous Parisian Garden of
Plants, from which he received stimulation for the
notable essay he was soon to write. He called on literary
men of Europe, particularly Scotland's Carlyle and England's Wordsworth. To America he returned with improved health, a brighter outlook on life, and a determination to make his contribution to literature.

Having departed from freshly beaten paths of thought,
Emerson was obliged to seek other routes or make his
own. He had faith in his ideas and dedicated himself to
the task of presenting them to the world. The quiet
village of Concord became his chosen place of residence.
For a number of years he continued preaching wherever
called; lectured every winter in Boston on literature,

history, or other subjects of general cultural value; conducted a life-long correspondence with Thomas Carlyle; wrote poetry, and established a reputation as a thoughtful man. His lecture engagements steadily increased until they covered a considerable portion of the United States and extended to Scotland and England.

As a college student, Emerson gathered ideas by much reading and thinking in channels of his own choosing. As a teacher, he used his spare time in reflection on problems unrelated to his routine work. As a minister, he set forth his ideas from the pulpit. As lecturer, he widened his scope and spread his ideas to the inhabitants of the villages, towns, and cities of many states. And finally, as poet and essayist, he utilized the literary art in recording for all time twenty-two volumes of written ideas.

The powerful influence of ideas upon human character and conduct makes necessary a clear knowledge of their significance and adds seriousness to their use. Such usage involves the passing on of the recorded experience of the race; it necessitates searching through books, libraries, and unpublished documents; it demands by the fire of thought the creation of new ideas, the transformation and reorganization of the old, and correctly applying all to the problems of life. Moreover, there must be an interpretation in the light of truth as revealed in the Bible. Likewise the source and nature of ideas must be known.

Many of Emerson's ideas were acquired through extensive study. He explored the fields of English literature and philosophy, walked the trails of German thinkers, and found refuge in the wisdom of the Greeks. In the writings of Plato and the Neo-Platonists he discovered a mine of thought and the core of his own philosophy. After having traversed the most fertile literary and philosophic regions of Europe, he caught sight of more distant shores that entranced his intellectual soul and enraptured him through his middle and later years. Early he had cast a longing look beyond the confines of western culture into the distant, hazy Orient, where humanity and civilization were born and where world literature originated. Upon exploring this land of mystery, he found that the ideas of antiquity fitted well into his own. Hindu philosophy gave him particular pleasure, and Persian poetry afforded poetic stimulation. The ideas of the Orient were transmitted into various essays and thus introduced to American culture.

The essays and poems of the Concord sage, an idealist who was himself the ideal of thoughtfulness, contain many gems of truth and beauty. There are shining thoughts on love and friendship, art and nature, character, manners, heroism, education, morals, books and literature, originality, and immortality. Thoughts on self-reliance and self-respect are there, which inspire men to do their best.

But there are other ideas that do not please and satisfy. The author declared that every man had personal and direct access to the God within him and implied that there was no need of a divine mediator, Jesus Christ. He wrote much about religion and referred often to Jesus but excluded the crucifixion and resurrection. He respected Christ as a teacher but was not interested in Him as a Redeemer who took upon Himself the sins of the world. Christ he did not consider more divine than other men, although he reverenced Him for His stainless life. Scripture was considered merely a guide, which was to him no more authoritative than one's own experience. The Christian idea of heaven was attacked, and in fact Christianity assailed. The emphasis on the goodness of human nature, while at the same time ignoring evil, may be attractive, but is contrary to the facts of life.

The prominent American poet and essayist has influenced creative writing and stimulated minds by bringing new materials for thought. He has contributed to the study of comparative religion and comparative literature. American scholarship has been encouraged; but likewise has modern religious liberalism, an enemy of true Christian progress.

XVI

AT THE SHRINE OF BACCHUS *

ROBERT HERRICK

THERE is an idol, at once among the most modern and the most ancient of gods, that men ardently embrace. The history of this god is almost as old as the history of man, for already in the antediluvian age, especially in the days when Noah was building an ark, and again in the days of Sodom, men were worshipers at this shrine. When the great kingdom of Babylon was in its glory, Belshazzar made a notable feast to a thousand of his lords and drank wine with them from the golden goblets taken from God's holy temple in Jerusalem. This occasion, made dramatic and horrible by the appearance of an unknown hand writing the king's doom on the wall, has been vividly pictured by the poets, especially by Heinrich Heine. In the fashionable society of mighty Rome the luxury-loving citizens and the gifted poets were devoted worshipers of this god. And in our modern world, including America and nearly all the Christian nations, the glory of this attractive idol has not departed.

The idols that stood solemnly in the temples of the heathen nations of antiquity, having been made from metal, stone, or wood by human hands, could neither hear nor act and were completely powerless. In the days of Elijah the prophets of Baal called most desperately from morning until evening and leaped and cut themselves until the blood gushed over their bodies, but there

* Bacchus was the Roman god of wine.

was not the slightest response, for they had an external
and a lifeless god. But it is not so with the popular idol,
Wine. He is an internal god, a god who enters into the
body, the blood, and the life of the worshiper, and acts
with a quick and fiery power.

This jealous but deceptive god shines and sparkles in
the goblet, its gorgeous colors please the eye, and there
is a charming sweetness to the palate. But "at the last
it biteth like a serpent, and stingeth like an adder." It
has been the conviction of the best people on earth, as
well as the pronouncements of God, that despite his
radiant, dazzling attractions, this is not a safe nor profitable god to worship, for he is cruel and revengeful and
follows the worshiper with relentless scourges and plants
bitter stings in his breast. The wise man, Solomon, was
not misinformed as to the effects of this human enemy
and ally of Satan. "Who hath woe? who hath sorrow?
who hath contentions? who hath babbling? who hath
wounds without cause? who hath redness of eyes? They
that tarry long at the wine; they that go to seek mixed
wine."

Among the devotees to this god have been many of the
gifted and intelligent. The poets especially have found
pleasure in his influence, have composed songs of praise
in his honor and made the merry tavern ring with sensu-
ous bacchanalian verses. Even Shakespeare, although
quoting the Bible in his dramatic productions, was fond
of the cup, and according to records accepted as reliable,
died in consequence of drinking. One young man in
particular who reached exalted heights in bacchanalian
lyrics was Robert Herrick. He had been in youth an
apprentice to his uncle, a jeweler to the king. Then,
after completing an academic career at Cambridge Uni-

versity, he lived for a period of twelve years in London. Like numerous poets before and after him, he became associated with London tavern life and acquired hosts of friends among noblemen and wits, men of law and letters. In taverns, centers of social life, he drank wine with Ben Jonson and his fellow poets and became a leader in the revelry. At the merry feasts, Herrick, believing the wine-god was a ministering spirit to the muses, drank healths to his favorite pagan poets, Homer, Virgil, Ovid, and Catullus.

During this gay period of London life Herrick, lover of wine and song, not only indulged in the frolic of the taverns, but devoted his bright talents to glorifying the pleasures of the cup and to composing classic odes for worship at the shrine of Bacchus. In his "Farewell to Sack" he bid a reluctant farewell to the idol which, he says, had been nearer and dearer to him than kindred or friend, than the soul to the body, or almost any other pleasure on earth, an idol that shines more radiantly than sunbeams in summer. While bidding farewell to sack, his favorite wine, he bestows upon it the most lavish praise. He says he has found it able to control grief, despair, and vexation, and to make the blood as active as a flash of lightning, and that it has filled great poets like Horace with fire and flame. With admiration he gazes upon it, disregarding utterly the proverbial advice, "Look not thou upon the wine when it is red, when it giveth his color in the cup, when it moveth itself aright." In his farewell Herrick still admires and loves this idol, but has found it too powerful for his brain and has been forced to leave it; his poetry must now be written without the help of this strong assistant.

In another exalted ode, "The Welcome to Sack," the poet in the most extravagant terms welcomes his god, Wine, whose radiant flame outglares the sun. He refers to wine as his saint, he being "her fierce idolator." He adoringly implores his "illustrious idol" as a living god. Desire and love have been intensified by absence from his god, which is now more welcome to him than is the happy soil to the sea-scourged voyager. Between Herrick and his wine there is an Anthony and Cleopatra relation, a lover's attitude, and he adoringly confesses his fierce love. He had for a time left this god in order to confirm his zeal and double his affection, and now he returns to the power that can make him more active and nimble and add to his genius.

After twelve years of London life, a revolution occurred in the career of Herrick. He had been interested in law but now decided to enter service in the Church. There was at this time a vacancy in Dean Prior, which is a church in Devonshire; the position was accepted by the poet, and he exchanged the gay society of London to become pastor in a village community. He resolved to bid farewell to secular poetry and devote his muse to pious verse. The large church in which he served as a minister stood in a quiet, secluded spot at the end of a country lane, and with a few exceptions was attended by unlettered farmers. Being sometimes lonely and discontented in Devonshire, he perhaps often longed for the cheerful association with London friends; he, however, devoted himself to his calling as a minister and found some delight in the country pleasures and village customs. Generously he sympathized with the people in their funerals and composed songs for their marriages and country festivals.

Although Herrick as a minister seems to have manifested a childlike trust in God and a recognition of Christ as man's redeemer and expressed his faith clearly and simply in poetry and taught his people repentance for sin and the goodness of God, he has been characterized, perhaps incorrectly, as a pagan at heart. Had he destroyed his early secular poetry as did Herbert, he might not have become branded by scholars and known to posterity as a pagan. His secular songs are so much more numerous than the sacred and so perfect in literary qualities, that it has been difficult to look upon him as a saint. However sincere and pious he may have been as a minister, he has left on record bacchanalian lyrics of high literary quality that have no Christian elements in them but are completely pagan in content and spirit. They do no credit to a Christian minister. He lived, of course, in a day when the tavern was the center of social life, when heavy drinking was common, and when drunkenness was a prevailing vice. But one feels that if Robert Herrick had spent his early years in a pious Christian manner, he would have become a greater preacher and a better man.

XVII

THE ART OF LOVING GOD — I

RICHARD ROLLE

THE MOST worthwhile thing a person can do in this world, according to the profound conviction of Richard Rolle, is to love God. In comparison with this, no other goal deserves striving for. To succeed in so great a task, Rolle was willing to forsake home and friends, earthly possessions and pleasures, to be a wanderer, to be ridiculed and considered a fool, to despise the world, and to seek to love God with all his heart and soul and might. Advancement for himself alone in this great art was not sufficient; he was impelled to attract others to the duty and pleasure of loving God.

Richard Rolle was born about the year 1300 in Yorkshire, northern England, and died during the great plague in 1349. After elementary schooling, he was sent to Oxford, where he was maintained by a wealthy archdeacon, Thomas Neville, for his parents were too poor to support him at the university. Being in disagreement with the religious situation and teachings at Oxford, he left at the age of eighteen after some years attendance there and decided to devote himself to a religious career in his own way. He left his home and parents to become a hermit. He went to a church where he prayed so earnestly that the wife of John de Dalton was impressed. From the priest he obtained consent to preach the next day, and by his eloquent sermon pleased John de Dalton, who invited him home for dinner. Dalton was the outstanding man of that community. His sons, who were home from Oxford, identified the youth as Richard Rolle, son of William Rolle, a special friend of John de Dalton's. When dinner was finished, Rolle wished to leave, but Dalton prevented him, and after the others were gone held a private conversation with him. Learning that the young man wished to be a hermit, Dalton clothed him with suitable garments and arranged to have him stay in a cell in his house.

While in this cell, Rolle had a critical temptation. There was a conflict in his life between earthly love and the continuance of his devotion to Jesus. A beautiful young woman, perhaps belonging to the Dalton circle, was the source of the temptation; but he overcame, and his devotion to his Master was strengthened. He felt that the blood of Jesus was his aid, and from that time on sought more fully to love Jesus.

After two years and nine months with the Dalton family, he decided to leave. Since his cell was near a storehouse, and from May to November there was a continual passing of heavy carts used in storing the grain, there was not sufficient quietness for spiritual contemplation. Furthermore, he was not treated with the same consideration as formerly and complained of having received moldy bread. Dalton had become dissatisfied with the young man who had left preaching and public work for the sake of contemplation.

During these first, nearly three, years as a hermit, Rolle had made great spiritual advancement. He found delight in prayer and meditation, and his whole desire was on things celestial. The heavenly door was opened, he experienced a revelation of the divine purpose for his life, and was impelled to wander and preach and write.

It is thought that at this time he went to France, where he received at the University of Paris special training in theology and an enthusiasm for the interpretation of Scripture.

A year after leaving his cell at the Dalton home, Rolle sat one night in a chapel and found great delight in the softness of prayer and meditation. Suddenly he felt a strange heat which, he discovered, came from the Creator. An increasing love for God was burning in his soul, and this "heat of eternal love" proved an outstanding experience in his spiritual progress.

Nine months later, he sat in the same chapel singing psalms, and praying, with his whole desire intent on celestial things. On this occasion, he had an experience he describes as follows: "I felt within me a melodious harmony, and received from heaven the most delectable symphony, which remained with me in mind. For my thought was continually changed into melodious song, and I had, as it were, songs in meditation, and even in my very prayers and psalmody I uttered the same sound. Thenceforth, through the affluence of eternal sweetness I burst out into singing what I had formerly spoken— privately, however, because only before my Creator." These rare spiritual events through which Rolle advanced wonderfully in the love of God he found difficult to describe, but, using the language of the senses, referred to them as "heat, sweetness, and light."

The supreme degree of the love of Christ was attained through these experiences. Rolle believed none will receive similar experiences but those who especially love the name of Jesus and so honor that name that they will never permit it to leave memory except in sleep. Though he felt he could not adequately describe his experiences in coming to the fire of love, he defined it briefly a "rapture by the raising of the mind to God through con templation." In this manner he was made a mystic which is the great subject of his writings. He attained this spiritual height by the time he was twenty-three years of age.

Getting to know God became the most important busi ness of his life. He was determined to follow his call a he saw it and had become a hermit against the wishes o parents and friends. To the rules of any religious orde he would not submit but made his own rules. He became dead to the world but alive unto God. He chose the solitary life; "to sit by himself alone" was the way fo him. Great joy was found in contemplation, and he said "In this world God's lovers are drunken in the wonderfu sweetness of contemplation." Although he believed preaching and contemplation incompatible, yet he fel that he must go forth and tell the world of the love o God. He saw that it was necessary to teach his fellow and solved the problem to some extent by occasionally changing the place of his hermitage. Ecclesiastica authorities, however, prevented his preaching, so he made written expositions of Scripture and spread abroad his message in writings.

Rolle was sensitive to criticism and has referred in his writings to unkindness, slander, and persecution. Falsely he was judged and maligned, he says, because he con versed with the carnal, was at home with the rich, and spoke to all classes of people about the Christian faith "My enemies sought to have me thrown as a scamp ou of the houses in which I was loved." They tried to dis cover error in his teaching. Some who had been his best friends became his worst persecutors. Sometimes he was a friendless wanderer and took his food at gates with beggars. To some he appeared a madman.

For a time he lived in a remote cell on the estate of a wealthy lady, who, with her husband, supported him for some years. Finally he settled near the nunnery at Hampole, where the latter years were spent as a counsellor to the nuns and all who came to him.

He was also a severe critic of others and attacked the worldly rich and the learned. He reproached contemporary monks and bitterly arraigned contemporary priests. The clergy were blamed for lack of spirituality and for ignorance of the sacred Scriptures. His works are full of condemnation of the worldliness of clerics, secular and regular. From all dedicated to the service of the church he strictly demanded poverty and freedom from worldly concerns. Some of his writings show a special interest in improving the parish clergy. The preaching work and love of poverty of the Franciscan friars were praised.

To Richard Rolle, God was real, more real than any material thing in this world. He knew God and experienced God. The loss of all things he voluntarily suffered that he might win Christ and know Him and the fellowship of His sufferings. Nothing was able to separate him from the love of God, and the love for God to which he attained in the highest degree.

XVIII

THE ART OF LOVING GOD — II

RICHARD ROLLE

The reader should remember that the ideals of Richard Rolle, wherein solitude, poverty, celibacy, and other aspects of asceticism are advocated, may be found unsuitable for the changed conditions of modern life. His attitude and many of his practices are still commendable, however.

TO REACH the highest degree of love for God, Richard Rolle chose the path of self-surrender, contemplation, and solitude. But he was more than a hermit. Seeing the great need of leading others to the same blessed experiences with God, he was also a missionary. Having as a layman no ecclesiastical authority for preaching, he from youth sent forth his messages in writing. He was a mystic according to the definition: "The mystic is a man whose entire life is wrapped up in, and saturated with, the love of God." His experiences are characterized as mystical and his writings as setting forth the doctrines of mysticism. In his earlier years he wrote in Latin, but later he had disciples who could read only English, so he wrote some of his best treatises in the vernacular. The main theme of his writings is the love of God.

Love is a deliberate stirring of our thought toward God and makes us one with God. Love is a desire of the heart, a burning longing for God, a coupling together of the loving and the loved. The heart of a true lover of Jesus Christ is turned into the fire of love and burns in love and makes one so shine in virtues that no part of him may be dark in vices. The person who loves God sets all his thoughts on God and forsakes the world solely for the love of God. He is delighted to be counted worthy to suffer pain for the love of Christ. When one loves God perfectly he is not disturbed by any word that men may say.

In order for one to love God there must be a conversion, or turning to God, for the love is not found in a sinful heart. Turning to God is turning from the world, from sin, and from the devil. The person who has turned to God avoids any word, deed, or sight tending to evil. For the cleansing of the sins of the heart one needs sorrow of heart. For the sins of the mouth confession of mouth is needed. To be cleansed from sins of deed there must be fasting, prayer, and almsdeeds. To turn from the world is to forget all idle and worldly occupations, to suffer gladly for God so that one's soul is wholly turned to God and dead to all things that are sought and loved in the world. Incessant thinking upon His counsel and His commandments helps to achieve turning to God.

The lover of God must despise the world. One despises the world when he does not love it. To despise this world is to go through life without loving temporal and passing things; to seek nothing but God. Compel yourself to despise the world, which is full of wretchedness, malice, persecution, wrath, and lust. Count riches as nothing and do not glory in physical beauty. It is enough to love God, to praise God, to be with God, to rejoice in God. You may have your choice: If you love the world, you will perish with it; if you love Christ, you will reign with Him.

When one turns wholly to God, the devil tries to deceive in a thousand ways. One is in persuading people to abstain too much from food and sleep. Rolle, believing in moderation and reasonableness, refers often to the imprudence and danger of excessive abstinence. Too much abstinence from food and sleep makes one too feeble for doing God's work and prevents one from thinking and praying effectively. "When young eat and drink; later when thou knowest better thyself and God, abstinence is more proper."

There is no sin in wealth, but in the use of it, and in the heart's desire concerning it. Rolle believed that it is possible to love God and have wealth. Poverty in itself is no virtue, and they who willingly are poor but lack meekness and lowliness are more wretched than they who are rich. But he saw great blessings in poverty and considered it a help in loving God. One must forsake all things that might hinder and must set his desire only in the glory of his Maker. To follow Christ in poverty is a part of forsaking the world. Those who have no comfort in this world but give their hearts entirely to God and seek nothing but Him, God comforts wonderfully. Those who love God find joy in suffering for God; through the help of God, they desire no earthly thing.

One must remember that our life here is but a moment when compared with eternity; our ending here is uncertain for we know not when nor where we shall die; and we must answer before the righteous Judge how we have lived and what we have done. Only those are holy who hate sin and despise all earthly things, who never cease from good works, who love Jesus Christ, and whose whole desires are set on heaven. If one loves poverty and despises the riches of this world, he shall have riches without end. To love God wisely one must expend all his might in God's service. Shepherds found Jesus in a crib between beasts; we also must seek Him in the way of poverty.

Solitude offers great advantages for the lover of God. To forsake the solace and joy of the world, enter a solitary life, suffer tribulation and anguish here, may appear painful to men, "but we have more joy and more true delight in a day than they have in the world all their lives." The special gift of those who live a solitary life is to love Jesus Christ. One can love God best when least occupied with the business of this world. Rolle felt that when sitting, he loved God more than when standing or walking. He then was most at rest, and one can best love God when most at rest in body and soul.

There is value in silence. Vain and ill speech shows that one is without the grace of God. To speak little helps in loving God.

Rolle writes much about the joy contemplation brings. In the contemplative life one forsakes the world and all its vanity and lusts; he gives himself up wholly to prayer and meditation and to loving God. The active life is more in danger because of the temptations that are in the world. Although he considered the contemplative higher than the active, and necessary for his own perfection, he recognized that one may live godly in an active life. In the active one must provide his household with the necessaries of life. Acts of mercy are involved: feeding the hungry, giving drink to the thirsty, clothing the naked, giving shelter to the homeless, and visiting the sick and those in prison. The contemplative life is more enduring, more restful, more delectable and lovelier. There is a yearning for the things of heaven and wonderful joy in God's love. All obstacles between one's mind and God are removed. The door of heaven is opened, and the glory of God is seen. Before the sweetness of contemplation there must be weeping and sorrow, a complete forsaking of the vanities of the world. The contemplative person loves solitude that he may be hindered by no man. Solitaries reach the highest perfection, but those who also fulfill the office of a preacher surpass those who are given only to godly things and not to the needs of their neighbors.

In contemplation, there is fellowship with God through reading the Scriptures, prayer, and meditation. It is good to meditate on the suffering of Christ and His death, to think of what He suffered for our salvation in wandering and preaching, in hunger, thirst, cold, heat, and in the cursings and revilings of men. Steadfast thinking on the suffering and death of Christ moves one to desire God's love and the joys of heaven and to despise the vanities of this world.

To be successful in prayer is to seek and ask of God night and day, with all earthly thoughts removed, finding comfort only in God. At first it may seem hard to take one's heart from all earthly things, but when once touched with the sweetness of heaven, a person will have little desire for the mirth of this world. When one's heart is wholly ordered to the service of God, one will wish to steal away alone for prayer and meditation. Through good thoughts and holy prayers one's heart will be made burning in the love of Jesus Christ.

Constantly Rolle stresses the value of the study of the Word of God. He desired to increase interest in the Bible and wrote numerous commentaries. He insisted that he was directly taught by God, and was inspired in understanding the Bible. His translation of the Psalms into

English became the orthodox version during the four-
teenth and fifteenth centuries and influenced later translations. His commentaries brought him persecution, but
finally the church approved of his Scriptural interpretation. Reading the Scriptures, said Rolle, is a great aid
to him who seeks the love of God, who seeks to be kindled
with the desire for heavenly joys and to despise earthly
things. Such reading helps one to know his faults, to
know what is sin, and what one should do and what not.

One of the most constant elements in his writings is
praise of the holy name of Jesus. At that time Mary, the
mother of Jesus, was the object of worship, but Rolle did
not choose to center his devotion upon the virgin. He
recognized Jesus as the Son of God, the source of comfort
and power, and he definitely broke from the prevailing
Mariolatry, devoting his life to praise of the holy name
of Jesus. No aspect of his teaching had a greater influence; the cult of the Holy Name of Jesus sprang up
all over Europe during the latter Middle Ages. By thinking on the name Jesus one can overcome the world, said
Rolle.

Included in his writings against love of the world is
love of dress. If your dress shows that you have forsaken
the world, that you have no delight in earthly things,
that you are in God's service, your heart should be what
your appearance shows. Not all are holy who wear the
dress of holiness, and it is a shame to appear to men
better than one really is. When you love God you will
not desire many garments and dainties, only such as you
need. Thus Rolle wrote to the Yorkshire nuns whom he
tried to spiritualize and who had to be admonished continually because of their gay clothes. In some of the
houses of nuns discipline was lax.

"Busy" is a word often occurring in his writings. When one loves God he will not be idle but will be busy thinking of God, speaking of God, praying, doing good, working profitable things. He will change his thoughts from the world and center them wholly on God. He will change his mouth from worldly speech and speak of Christ. He will change his hands from works of vanity to work for Christ.

In his own experience, Richard Rolle attained to the highest degree of love, and in his writings has a number of times described three degrees:

"Love is truly insuperable when it may not be overcome by any other desire, when for Christ a man freely casts off all hindrances, when he quenches all temptations and fleshly desires, and when he suffers patiently all burdens for Christ and is overcome by no flattery or pleasure.

"Love is truly inseparable when the mind is kindled with great love and drawn to Christ with undivided thought, when one does not for a single moment allow Him to pass out of mind, but as one is bound to Him in heart one thinks of Him, sighs for Him, cries to be held with His love. . . .

"Love ascends to a singular degree when it excludes all comfort but that which is in Jesus, when nothing but Jesus may suffice. The soul set in this degree loves Him alone; it thirsts only for Christ, yearns for Christ, pants with sole desire for Him; for Him it sighs, in Him it burns, and in Him alone it rests."

XIX

BEAUTY INVISIBLE

NATHANIEL HAWTHORNE

NOT FAR does one need to travel in the realm of words or experience to become familiar with the idea of beauty. The eye reveals what is the appearance of a flower, a tree, or a face that is beautiful, and other organs and faculties also contribute to an understanding. Yet the concept of beauty is one the wisest men ponder long over and find difficult to define. What is beautiful to you may not be so to me. Then, too, beauty may dwell where most do not discern it. The supreme literary artist, Hawthorne, found beauty where many would find only monotony and emptiness: he found it in silence, in sadness, in solitude, in a customhouse, on a farm, and in outcast people.

It is unusual and really unnatural to see a healthy youth find values in such a strange environment. The explanation involves a chamber in a Salem house where a rare human being sat and mused and meditated. He had early seen sorrow, for his mother had withdrawn herself into a secluded room and for forty years mourned the loss of her husband, who died when Nathaniel Hawthorne was but four years of age. And so, as has been said, he may never have seen the face of his mother without a sadness even in her smile. Furthermore, from nine to twelve he could not participate in outdoor games on account of an injury to his foot that occurred while he was playing ball. The time was improved in wide reading.

A delightful year was spent in the new wild lands of Maine, where the family resided in a large house near the shores of Sebago Lake. The few houses of the village were surrounded with dense primeval forests through which the boy often wandered with gun in hand. In moonlight nights of winter he often skated on the lake alone with the icy White Mountains rising in the distance. The delight and freedom of those days were never forgotten, although they intensified his habits of solitude. "The grand heritage of nature was around him, and he sought out its most secret haunts of beauty and unbroken silence, while in his heart and at his home there was the loneliness of sorrow." Thus the gloom of the woods cast their shadow over him.

But it was time to go to college, so Hawthorne had to abandon his beloved Maine woods and return to Salem, Massachusetts, in order to finish his precollegiate training. There he studied, dreamed about Sebago, and soon entered Bowdoin College. Bowdoin, situated in the small rural village of Brunswick, Maine, gave him three valuable friends—Franklin Pierce, Horatio Bridge, and Henry W. Longfellow. His record there was somewhat marred by card playing and drinking. With Horatio Bridge he often wandered through the pine woods and watched the logs tumble along the current of the Androscoggin.

After college, Hawthorne went back to his childhood home at Salem on the seashore and began his twelve-year term of seclusion. The house with very common-place surroundings was not a pleasing one. It faced one of the quietest streets in any New England town. On the second floor, Hawthorne occupied a room that has been described as a "little, dark, dreary apartment under the eaves." In this house also lived his mother and two sisters, Elizabeth and Louisa. They lived apart and seldom ate at a common table. Hawthorne often had his meals brought to him. During the day he was shut up alone in his room, but when evening came and darkness enveloped the earth he plunged forth into the night through the town and beyond. At nightfall a gloomy sense of unreality depressed his spirits and impelled him to go and satisfy himself that the world consisted of more than shadowy materials. An unknown figure, he passed on through the darkness, perhaps met some luckless lovers or the mail coach, and saw the peacefully illuminated firesides. And thus the silence and solitude of the day were reenforced by the gloom and dreariness of night rambles.

At intervals he sought the solitude of the seashore or the forest in an all-day excursion. His soul communed with the shore and sea and sky as he traversed the broad spaces of sand, clambered over crags, watched the struggling waves, the sea birds, marine plants and animals, or whatever his keen eyes could light upon. And when he went back to town he did not go as a misanthrope; although an onlooker rather than an associate, he was the friend of man.

Most of the daytime during those twelve years of seclusion was devoted to meditation, imaginative thinking, reading, and writing. He thought about New England and its Puritanism, about his ancestors and the past, about evil and destiny. The early life of New England provided material for stories, many of which he destroyed because of the disinterestedness of publishers. Out of silence and solitude intermingled with the elements of sadness an imaginative intellect created tales of surpassing beauty. The little room where this took place he afterwards called a haunted chamber wherein thousands of visions appeared to him. He considered it significant because there his mind and character were formed, there he was sometimes hopeful and sometimes despondent, and there he wasted much of his youth.

The silence of those years was sad, mysterious, pleasant, and potent. It was a silence that rolled back the curtains of time and presented visions of the eternal soul of man. It was a silence that permitted genius to unfold itself in artistic expression ever praised for its remarkable beauty. And it was a silence tinged with gloom. The most beautiful scenes are not always those flooded with the brightest sunlight. Twilight and gathering darkness touch the landscape with a sweet sobriety and the meditative soul with sadly solemn thoughts. Hawthorne in those lonely years of youth felt the gentle stroke of mild-eyed melancholy and the flowers that blossomed in the garden of his early literature have a pale tint. He himself said that his early tales should be read in the clear brown twilight in which they were written.

Finally Hawthorne found beauty in solitude. Solitude gave opportunity for reflection, for companionship with nature and his own thoughts, and for the free growth of his stories. It made possible youthful meditation, which strengthens character and develops one's philosophy of life. It furnished an environment wherein his thought and imagination could find expression in an exceedingly beautiful style and where something of the beautiful could be discerned in darkness and mystery. It enabled him to keep the dew of his youth and the freshness of his heart.

Visions of invisible beauty rekindled by a glowing imagination were not limited to the period of youth nor to one lonely, haunted chamber. After winning fame through successful writing of tales, and happiness through friendship with Sophia Peabody, Hawthorne during two years weighed coal and salt on dingy schooners in Boston harbor.

On bleak and dirty vessels where Irishmen shoveled and wheeled coal and where the grimy unshaven cook washed dishes in dirty water, the writer of tales toiled all day and in the evening walked to his residence with coal streaks on his face. Willingly he was chained to work, for he believed that these experiences would later add truth and wisdom to his literary productions. Though on dirty schooners in a dismal dock, the coal dust did not blind his eyes to the glories of earth and sky nor deaden his sensations to the delightful breezes that kissed his brow. Sometimes he saw the large and brilliant segment of a rainbow in the sky, or resplendent floating clouds so glorious and so lovely that he "had a fantasy of heaven's being broken into fleecy fragments and dispersed throughout space, with its blessed inhabitants yet dwelling blissfully upon those scattered islands."

One cold, bleak day he was plagued by two sets of coal shovelers for whom he had to measure coal at the same time. The magic gift of fancy enabled him to feel that he was not half frozen by the bitter wind nor tormented by sooty coal heavers but was "basking quietly in the sunshine of eternity." So if he did sacrifice several years in the dungeon of a customhouse, he was never deprived of exquisite and beautiful images that revealed beauty and truth invisible to others.

Farm work was to Hawthorne a sort of bondage that checked his thinking and his writing, a thraldom of heart and mind, yet while working on Brook Farm he saw something of beauty there, particularly as expressed in nature. One morning, as recorded in his journal, he worked on a hillside under the clear blue sky, and it almost seemed as if he were at work in the sky itself.

While living in the country near Lenox, Massachusetts, he was walking one day to the village when he saw the face of a beautiful woman gazing at him from a cloud. The vision, or cloud picture, lasted only a moment, but long enough for him to note its elegance and pleasant expression of countenance. If he could see so beautiful a face in a cloud it is not surprising that, on the side of a mountain where immense rocks were thrown together in a symmetrical manner, he could see the noble and glorious features and the grand and sweet expression of a Great Stone Face.

Men and women interested Hawthorne above everything else, and he was able to see something admirable in the lowest outcast. While visiting his friend, Bridge, at Augusta, Maine, he saw there a queer Frenchman, small, ungainly, ill dressed, and insignificant in appearance. But he did not ignore him; on the contrary he respectfully conversed with him, gave him credit for his intelligence, and admired his lively talk. He had sympathy for the unfortunate Frenchman's limitations and dissatisfactions. On another occasion he met a one-armed soap maker, a grim, grizzly, black-bearded, beastly figure, disagreeable looking, bare-footed, and very badly dressed. Might it not be easy for a sensitive artist to despise such a character? Hawthorne listened to his conversation, recognized a certain courtesy in his manner, and observed an acuteness of judgment and a cultivated mind. He did not think it proper for people to scorn this man who had not wholly lost self-respect. The most humble or insignificant person had virtues which might be altogether invisible to the ordinary observer.

To be able to see values in adversity and to find beauty in unattractive or commonplace surroundings is an asset. It is well to look beneath the mere surface of things and to find hidden gems of gold. But too often standards of beauty are wrong and what is considered beautiful is really not so. Hawthorne was a descendant of the Puritans, but was not in sympathy with their religion and was repelled by it rather than attracted to it.

XX

GLEANINGS FROM AN ANECDOTE MONGER

THOMAS FULLER

ALL over England went Thomas Fuller, clergyman, antiquarian, historian, and essayist, collecting information from all sorts of people for his notable literary works. Shortly after graduating from Cambridge he became a minister, preaching first in the town of Cambridge, then in Dorsetshire, and later in London, where he gained prominence rapidly as one of the great English preachers. He aimed especially to promote piety and made his sermons so interesting and attractive by anecdotes and witty illustrations that the people listened to him gladly, and thronged his services to the extent that there were as many outside the church as within. Because of the Civil War, which brought to him trials and difficulties, he was obliged to flee from London and eventually became a preacher to the king's soldiers. He continued his literary pursuits, and, while marching with the army from place to place, made historical and antiquarian researches, becoming acquainted with country people, laborers, the aged, and the learned, and with zeal and persistence collected information for his monumental works. His three chief pursuits in life were writing, preaching, and making friends.

After the Civil War, Fuller returned to London, but, being a royalist, and the Presbyterians now being in full power, he was for a time deprived of the pulpit and his public ministry. Later, however, he again preached, having been appointed to the rectory at Waltham, twelve miles from London. In the quiet village of Waltham he had a comfortable home, a devoted congregation, occasional opportunities for preaching to London audiences, and favorable conditions for continuing work on the *Church History of Britain* and *History of the Worthies of England.*

Upon the publication of the *Church History* he became one of the important literary figures in London but was also subject to the attack of critics who failed to see the high merits of the work. Peter Heylin wrote a book against Fuller's *History,* pointing out the defects in a fault-finding manner. Three or four months later Fuller replied with fairness and forbearance and closed his answer to Heylin with a most gracious letter beginning, "To my loving friend, Dr. Peter Heylin," and ending with, "Who knoweth but that God, in His providence, permitted, yea, ordered, this difference to happen betwixt us, not only to occasion a reconciliation, but to consolidate a mutual friendship betwixt us during our lives, and that the survivor (in God's pleasure only to appoint) may make favorable and respectful mention of him who goeth first to his grave, the desire of him who remains, Sir, a lover of your parts, and an honorer of your person." Heylin failed to show a willingness to meet the proposal, and wrote a reply to Fuller's appeal. Fuller closed the quarrel by going to Heylin's lodgings and seeking his friendship, which the latter finally gave.

Thomas Fuller has been referred to as one of the "truest wits that ever lived," and as "the prime anecdote monger of the seventeenth century, and a capital story-teller." *The Holy State and the Profane State* is one of his most popular books, and consists of a series of essays presenting model characters, such as the good school-master, the good merchant, the faithful minister, etc. In these short essays are many wise sayings, pious instructions, and pleasant anecdotes. Among the wise sayings are such as: "He whose own worth doth speak, need not speak his own worth"; "Cheerfulness in doing renders a deed more acceptable"; "A lazy hand is no argument of a contented heart"; "As stout champions of truth follow in the rear as ever marched in the front"; "He that falls into sin is a man; that grieves at it is a saint; that boasteth of it is a devil."

The wisdom and pious instructions of Fuller may be seen in such an essay, for instance, as "The Faithful Minister." The faithful minister is depicted as one who, after having been trained and given a pastoral charge, tries to win the love and good will of his congregation that his ministry may be more beneficial and effective. But "if pious living and painful laboring in his calling will not win their affections, he counts it gain to lose them." He is grave and courteous to his people, but not too austere and retired. His sermons are very carefully prepared; he does not imitate those who can present sermons without study. He preaches from his heart as well as from his head and tells the people what they may do as well as what they may not do. In reproof he "whips the vice and spares the person." He quotes pertinent Scriptures and uses familiar illustrations but avoids a vain display of memory by excessive quotations and stories that may suggest bad thoughts to the hearers. His sermons are not too long nor is he as tedious as John Halsebach, professor at Vienna, who spent twenty-one years expounding the first chapter of Isaiah and did not have it finished then. God rewards the minister for his endeavor, not for his success.

Since the Church of England, of which Fuller was a member, held to a union of church and state, it was natural for him to write of the good soldier, the good general, and the wise statesman as important servants of the church. He considered the soldier called of God to his work, and having a lawful, necessary, commendable, and honorable profession; he says also that "our soldier knows that he shall possess the reward of his valor with God in heaven." He feels, however, that the occupation of a soldier is not for a Christian minister, and concludes, "nor suits it with my clergy-profession to proceed any further in this warlike description." Fuller, of course, presents high standards for these officials of the state and desires that in the holy state the statesman be an honest politician. One who believes in a separation of church and state and in the New Testament teachings on peace will not consider the profession of a soldier a proper one for the Christian. He will be nonresistant in times of peace and war and in all walks of life.

In addition to wise moral and religious counsels and celebrated definitions Fuller's *The Holy State and the Profane State* is especially attractive for its pleasant anecdotes and historical examples, some of which will be reproduced in the following paragraphs, including also the truths they are to illustrate.

Queen Catharine Dowager never kneeled on a cushion when she was at her devotions. A virtuous person is more careful of the heart than of the knees.

It is not good to be too curious in searching matters of no importance, in seeking hidden mysteries in useless questions. Captain Martin Frobisher brought from the farthest northern countries a ship's load of what he thought were mineral stones, but which were afterwards used to mend the highways.

When thrown unexpectedly into bad company, it may be necessary to be with them but not of them. The River Dee in Merionethshire, Wales, runs through Pimble Meer, but remains entire, and does not mingle her streams with the waters of the lake.

It is dangerous to jest with the Word of God or with the majesty of God. In the days of King Edward the Fourth a citizen in Cheapside was executed as a traitor for saying he would make his son heir to the crown. He only meant his own house, which had a crown for the sign.

Gallus Vibius was at first a man of great eloquence, and afterwards of great madness. He had so long mimically imitated madmen that he became one. "To make a trade of laughing at a fool is the highway to become one."

The faithful minister lives his sermons. It was said of one who preached very well and lived very ill, that "when he was out of the pulpit it was pity he should ever go into it, and when he was in the pulpit it was pity he should ever come out of it."

Bishop Andrews always had the picture of Mulcaster, his schoolmaster, over the door of his study to be his tutor and supervisor. It will help us to maintain a proper behavior by ever living as in the presence of God.

In order to maintain gravity one must avoid overmuch talk. A great talker, who took himself to be a grand wit, bragged that he was the leader of the discourse into whatsoever company he came. "None," said he, "dare speak in my presence, if I hold my peace." "No wonder," answered one, "for they are all struck dumb at the miracle of your silence."

A gentleman, traveling on a misty morning, asked a shepherd what the weather would be. "It will be what weather shall please me," said the shepherd. Being courteously requested to express his meaning, he answered, "Sir, it will be what weather pleases God, and what weather pleases God pleases me." Submission to God's will and pleasure makes for contentment in any circumstance.

If one has a good memory, he should not be vainly proud of it, but should thank God for it. Staupitius, tutor to Luther, and a godly man, made a vain display of his memory by repeating Christ's genealogy in Matthew I by heart in his sermon, but not being able to recall about the captivity of Babylon, he said, "I see God resisteth the proud," and so opened his book.

When our expectations fail, it is well to have patience and rely on God's providence, for He often provides for us above what we can think or desire. When Robert Holgate could not peaceably enjoy his small living in Lincolnshire, because of the quarrelsomeness of a neighbor, he went to London, where he came into the favor of King Henry VIII, and eventually was granted the archbishopric of York (one of the highest ecclesiastical positions in England).

Persons with deformed bodies sometimes have saintly souls. An emperor went by chance one Sunday into a church, where a most misshaped minister was conducting the service. The emperor scorned and condemned him, but when he heard him read, "for it is He that hath made us, and not we ourselves," he checked his proud thoughts, and made inquiry into the quality and condition of the man. On examination he found him to be most learned and devout, and so made him archbishop of Colen, a place he excellently filled.

Maud, mother of King Henry II, being besieged at Oxford in a cold winter, got away in the snow undiscovered by wearing white apparel. So some hypocrites, by professing a snowlike purity in their conversation, escape undiscerned by mortal eyes.

A famous Athenian soldier, Cynaegirus, caught hold of one of the enemy's ships. He held it first with his right hand, and when that was cut off, with his left; when both were cut off, he still kept it with his teeth. So the conscience of an evildoer or an atheist, though it be bruised, beaten, or maimed, still keeps him by the teeth, still feeds and gnaws upon him, and tortures and torments him.

In controversy a speedy answer may not be as sound as a slower one. When Melancthon, at the disputation of Ratisbon, was pressed with a shrewd argument by Eckius, he said, "I will answer you tomorrow." "Nay," said Eckius, "do it now, or it is nothing worth." "Yea," said Melancthon, "I seek the truth, and not mine own credit, and therefore it will be as good if I answer you tomorrow by God's assistance."

One should relieve his distressed kindred, but it is better to ease them in their profession than to ease them from their profession. A husbandman claimed that he was a relative of Robert Grosseteste, Bishop of Lincoln, and therefore requested that he be favored by having an office bestowed upon him. "Cousin," quoth the Bishop, "if your cart be broken, I'll mend it; if your plow old, I'll give you a new one, and seed to sow your land; but an husbandman I found you and an husbandman I'll leave you."

XXI

IS DEATH THE GOAL OF LIFE?

PERCY BYSSHE SHELLEY

I T IS noteworthy, in view of the fact that the poetry of Percy Bysshe Shelley was all produced in youth, that death, the defeater of physical life, high aims, and noble aspirations, stares grimly at the reader in nearly every poem. To Shelley, death seems the inevitable end after high endeavor, the only certain source of comfort and peace. Hope always fails, but death never. In "Alastor," a revealment of himself, death seems to have been the only permanent and satisfying achievement possible. Here the high-souled youth was blessed with nearly all possible natural advantages: beauty of figure and physique, intelligence, access to rich stores of knowledge, leisure for contemplation, and intimate association with all that is excellent, beautiful, and majestic in the natural world. He had not been corrupted by the sins of human society. He was brave and generous, "the gentle and beautiful child of grace and genius." The choicest impulses came to him from the sights and sounds of earth and air. From the great and good and lovely in philosophy of the past came to him knowledge and experience. The common sky and green earth stimulated in him love and wonder, and rare places of nature taught profound secrets. Travel among venerable ruins of ancient cities and countries, where he saw pyramids, ruined temples, and old writings on stone walls, illuminated his meditative mind with the secrets of the beginning of time. With all this marvelous equipment and experience, the magnanimous youth achieved nothing in this or any other world but death.

Whatever he may have experienced of peace and joy was of short duration. One night he had a vision of a maid who talked solemnly to him of knowledge, truth, virtue, liberty, and poetry, the very subjects in which he was most interested. As he was about to embrace her in love, the vision vanished from him. In his vision he had experienced a joy superior to what the real world had ever given him and felt that the only way to bring back his wonderful joy was to re-enter the realms of sleep in which state the vision had come to him. Apparently he could not do this. The failure to recover and re-experience love through his most satisfying vision stung him to despair, and he wandered all night in darkness through swamps and dells, bringing the appearance of death upon his cheek by the time morning dawned. Real joy could be found nowhere, so he wandered on day after day, his limbs becoming thinner and weaker. Some impulse urged him to the seashore, where the sight of a swan scaling the sky aroused in him a slight hope, which was at once followed by new reflections on the tragic wasting of his life and powers. That once soothing vision of love had come to him in sleep, and he felt convinced that only death, of which sleep is a symbol, held any charm for him. Near the shore he found a small, frail boat; this discovery impelled him to embark

And meet lone Death on the drear ocean's waste.

A whirlwind swept the boat on and on toward a destruction that seemed to please him, and he was finally driven into a dark, watery cavern. That sleep and death would not now keep him long from the vision of love gave him joy, for death had become the sole object of his search. After being delivered from the dark, winding cavern, his boat became involved in a treacherous whirlpool from which he was eventually saved by a wind. He then wandered on through grand scenes, soon following a winding stream through gorgeous forests and dells and coming finally to a silent and tranquil nook where no human step or voice had ever been heard before. Here he lay down on the brink of a chasm, placed his hand on an ivied stone, looked at the moon, and with calm and peaceful thoughts resigned

> *his high and holy soul*
> *To images of the majestic past.*

The present or future had nothing for him. Death at last brought peace to the unhappy youth. He had set out to search for truth and might properly have been satisfied with nothing short of immortality.

The high-souled youth sought perfection — perfect enjoyment, perfect love, perfect beauty, but found them not. He sought to find them in the natural world, but they can only be found in God, and Shelley never knew God nor believed in Him, "Who satisfieth the longing soul, and filleth the hungry soul with goodness." The youth is typical of Shelley himself, for the famous English poet soared high in the realms of idealism, looking longingly forward and gazing wildly backward, but never finding supreme joy. He followed a vain vision, seemingly beautiful, but remained forever sad and unsatisfied.

Shelley had ignored that which alone has the power to satisfy; therefore hope, peace, and satisfaction were lacking in his life. Because of burdens death seemed to him a balm for his weary soul and more desirable than life.

Yet now despair itself is mild,
  Even as the winds and waters are;
I could lie down like a tired child,
  And weep away the life of care
  Which I have borne and yet must bear,
  Till death like sleep might steal on me.

In his poetry, Shelley lamented the frailty of virtue, friendship, and love. His heart was filled with grief because joy had fled and he was left alone in the world. His rising hopes always collapsed, and he remained in hopeless grief and profound melancholy.

From Godwin's *Political Justice,* Shelley had early derived the idea that the established order is founded on oppression and that the two great tyrannies are the church and the state, religion and government. His acceptance of atheistic and revolutionary ideas caused the misery and unhappiness of his entire life. It resulted in his expulsion from college, making him in turn restless and antagonistic; it separated him from family and friends, for his father and mother had repudiated him; it harmed the sale of his works, which disheartened him so that the amount and quality of his writing was perhaps diminished. He considered the divine institution of marriage an enemy to human happiness and abandoned his first wife. His ideas of absolute liberty and his corresponding conduct made him so unpopular in England that he became an exile in Italy; there he suffered loneliness, for he had been deprived of his children as a result of his anti-christian beliefs.

The human heart of Shelley needed something to worship, so he dedicated his powers to and worshiped a god whom he called the Spirit of Beauty. He had great confidence in what this spirit could do for the world and for himself: he believed he was able and willing to free the world from dark slavery and to plant love in the human heart. Still he found a certain inconstancy in this god and found him unable to keep death from casting a gloom on the earth. The Spirit of Beauty did not have power over death, and therefore one could not put boundless and world-conquering faith in this god.

In certain notable poems, however, Shelley did rise above his melancholy reflections and found some hope in reality that death cannot destroy. A sensitive plant grew in a certain garden that flourished brilliantly with the most beautiful flowers and plants under the tender care of the lady of the garden. When the lady died, death entered the garden; consequently the fairest flowers all died and were supplanted with the loathsomest weeds. At length winter came, and these weeds, "which were forms of living death," also decayed, so that death seemed to reign supreme. Yet Shelley offers the conviction that the lady, the garden, and all the lovely flowers have really not passed away, that love and beauty do not die; he suggests that the soul of man is not completely annihilated at death.

The same idea of the unreality of death is presented in "Adonais," where the dead Keats is exalted to immortality. For the happy thought that Keats is alive and not dead is presented the gloomy conception that we are dead or in decay. There may be some ultimate consolation in the view that life is death and death is life, but there is little present comfort in such lines as the following:

> *we decay*
> *Like corpses in a charnel; fear and grief*
> *Convulse us and consume us day by day,*
> *And cold hopes swarm like worms within our*
> *living clay.*

Shelley believed that the soul of the departed Keats, as of any virtuous man, was at death made one with nature, with the Spirit of Love and Beauty, with the one eternal Spirit, and was present in all the lovely manifestations of nature.

Sometimes in his expressions of unsatisfied desire Shelley revealed imaginative visions of a sort of a pagan heaven, somewhat similar to what may be found in the folklore of ancient Irish literature, and which he described in the last section of "Lines Written Among the Euganean Hills," and in "Epipsychidion." In this otherworld of fairy tales and enchanted mountains, he imaginatively found supernatural delight, but having no theological conceptions of life and death and immortality that could withstand the assaults of doubt, he became submerged in melancholy when he reflected on such points.

Thus the poet, who had a passion for reforming the world, "ran wild over fields of ether," but never found a resting place. He chased falling stars but could never anchor his soul for long to a fixed one. Everything eluded his grasp, and he found nothing substantial. He uttered his cries of desire and despair and never found soul-satisfaction. His only certain refuge was death. Having never found God, he had not the Rock to build on, the Savior to give rest to his heavy-laden soul, nor the blessed hope of a bright immortality.

XXII

THE CONSECRATION OF TALENT

HARRIET BEECHER STOWE

I do not mean to live in vain. He has given me talents, and I will lay them at His feet well satisfied if He will accept them.

THIS decision expressed the mind of a New England girl, a daughter of the Puritans, Harriet Beecher Stowe. It was born out of soul struggles, for its author had passed through many a conflict, many a doubt. Harriet lived in a theological age and in a family where theology was the staff of life. Her father was Lyman Beecher, a minister and theologian. The atmosphere about her early life was one of spiritual and mental and emotional excitement, which deeply affected the sensitive, imaginative maiden.

Yet in her time of childhood she was not always unhappy. After the death of her mother, when Harriet was five years old, she spent happy days with her grandmother amid unfamiliar farm scenes near Guilford, Connecticut. At six she was back in the home of her father in Litchfield. He had remarried. She played with her younger brothers, rambling through the woods or rummaging in the garret. During these early years she loved to sit in a quiet corner of her father's study looking through whatever interesting books she could find. Her eyes had often scanned the titles of solemn theological treatises that reposed along the walls of that garret room far above the noise and confusion of the busy household. There was nothing very attractive or appropriate in those abstract works for a child, but one day her father brought home a large book that proved to be a source of great pleasure. It was Cotton Mather's *Magnolia*. In it she found many stories that told about the special providences of God in opening America to the settlement of the Pilgrim fathers. Her soul became filled with eagerness to do some great and valiant deed for her God and for her country.

The environment and influences of her childhood were such as to make her think much on religion. Long Sunday sermons reminded her of her sinfulness and the requirements for salvation. When in her thirteenth year, one beautiful summer morning Harriet stood at her open window viewing the grand scenes of nature. It was the morning of the holy Lord's day, but so resplendent with dewy freshness that she could scarcely feel herself a sinner. It was the Sunday for communion services, and her father at the church on this day preached about Jesus as the soul Friend offered to every human being. He spoke with deep feeling and in simple language, and with tenderness of a rich nature, concerning the generous love of Christ. The event of that day was described by Harriet in her own writings. It is reproduced as follows:

"Harriet sat absorbed. Her large blue eyes gathered tears as she listened, and when the minister said, 'Come, then, and trust your soul to this faithful Friend,' her little heart throbbed 'I will!' She sat through the sacramental service that followed with swelling heart and tearful eyes, and walked home filled with a new joy. She went up into her father's study and threw herself into his arms, saying, 'Father, I have given myself to Jesus and He has taken me.' He held her silently to his heart for a moment, and she felt his tears dropping on her head. 'Is it so?' he said. 'Then has a new flower blossomed in the kingdom this day!'"

It was after this that she passed through the darkest struggles. Her tender heart needed a loving God instead of the stern God preached by some of the New England clergy. Often she felt perfectly wretched and unhappy, but in her distress she called upon Jesus. At last, after passing most of her teen-age years in introspection and morbid sensitiveness, through seasons of depression and gloom, she fought through the storm and triumphed. She decided to put her religion to practice in a social way, to cultivate a spirit of kindness to everybody and become acquainted with all who would care to be acquainted with her. Hers now became the gospel of love—love for God, love for friends, love for humanity. Just as Jesus had accepted her life when she gave it to Him, so He now accepted her talents and used them unstintingly for the liberation of humanity.

God used the consecrated talents of Harriet Beecher Stowe in many ways. While a student in the school for girls conducted by her sister, Catharine, she began to render assistance in teaching. The Beecher family later moved to Cincinnati, where Lyman Beecher became president of a theological seminary, and where Harriet and her sister opened a school for the training of women teachers in anticipation of the establishment of public schools in the west. Here she produced her first published work, an elementary geography, and embarked on a literary career by writing for magazines. While living in this Ohio River city, she also acquired a first-hand knowledge of slavery, thus equipping her mind with the materials for her later anti-slavery literature.

At last the critical situation in her country and the grievous sufferings of a race made such an impression that she was aroused to the great work of her life. She wrote *Uncle Tom's Cabin* amid extraordinary household duties, for she had seven children, numerous guests, and many distractions. But she felt as if some divine power were urging her on and giving her the words to set down. The book was read by millions of people in hundreds of editions and translations in all parts of the world. The consecrated talent of a "wisp of a woman" did more than uproot the institution of slavery from its powerful hold upon a great nation. It produced a work that awakened the conscience of the world in behalf of weaker races and peoples, one which was an active agency in Christian evangelization and which revealed the power of the religion of Christ in enabling ignorant, oppressed individuals to rise from despair to triumph, from weakness to superhuman strength.

Harriet Beecher Stowe did not consecrate her talents and then sit down in idleness; nor did she wait in indolence and passivity until some committee or organization told her to do something. Her whirlwind energies she threw into whatsoever task she undertook, and she did not shrink from carrying out her deepest convictions. She wrote to stir the hearts of men and "to push on the movement of great causes in a turbid world." She was prompted by the burning conviction that she had a message for humanity, one of such supreme importance that it must be delivered without procrastination or apology and declared with all the emphasis that the combined powers of thought, emotion, and imagination could muster. All the vigor of an intense nature was employed in stripping the galling shackles from a downtrodden race. As a result her book has been designated "one of the greatest moral agencies the world has seen."

And is this all she did? What we have so far mentioned is a great deal; in fact, so much that one has said, "Few teachers and preachers can hope to accomplish such results as she did." But really she did more. *Uncle Tom's Cabin* is not the only book she wrote. There are thirty in all, consisting of religious stories which, in their delineation of New England life and character, tell how the brave Pilgrim fathers and mothers and children lived in the wilderness of the new world. These books of Harriet Beecher Stowe's are a treasure-house of good things. Then, too, she was something of a missionary. In Cincinnati, she had already taught Negro children, and, after the Civil War, for a number of years the family moved to Florida every autumn. There she spent her time going about doing good, giving her testimony for Christianity, and working to evangelize the region. With her own money she built a church and schoolhouse and herself taught colored children in the Sunday school. She contributed liberally to all kinds of private and public charities.

By consecrating her talents to Him who gave them, Harriet Beecher Stowe was abundantly rewarded. She became rich in love and all the Christian virtues and had the deep satisfaction of having honored God through service for humanity. With joy she could say that throughout life she had experienced "the intense, unwavering sense of Christ's educating, guiding presence and care."